Market A
in EC–US

CHATHAM HOUSE PAPERS

A European Programme Publication
Programme Director: Helen Wallace

The Royal Institute of International Affairs, at Chatham House in London, has provided an impartial forum for discussion and debate on current international issues for some 70 years. Its resident research fellows, specialized information resources, and range of publications, conferences, and meetings span the fields of international politics, economics, and security. The Institute is independent of government.

Chatham House Papers are short monographs on current policy problems which have been commissioned by the RIIA. In preparing the papers, authors are advised by a study group of experts convened by the RIIA, and publication of a paper indicates that the Institute regards it as an authoritative contribution to the public debate. The Institute does not, however, hold opinions of its own; the views expressed in this publication are the responsibility of the author.

CHATHAM HOUSE PAPERS

Market Access Issues in EC–US Relations

Trading Partners or Trading Blows?

Stephen Woolcock

The Royal Institute of International Affairs

Pinter Publishers
London

© Royal Institute of International Affairs, 1991

First published in Great Britain in 1991 by
Pinter Publishers Limited
25 Floral Street, London WC2E 9DS

British Library Cataloguing in Publication Data

A CIP catalogue record for this book is available from the British Library

ISBN 0-86187-082-4 (Paperback)
      0-86187-081-6 (Hardback)

Reproduced from copy supplied by
Koinonia Limited
Printed and bound in Great Britain by
Biddles Ltd

CONTENTS

ACKNOWLEDGMENTS

This volume forms the first of two publications from a research project on EC–US relations, undertaken by the European Programme of the Royal Institute of International Affairs under the direction of Dr Helen Wallace. A second Chatham House Paper is in preparation on the broader political dimensions of EC–US relations. This research has been carried out in association with the Council on Foreign Relations, New York, which has conducted two parallel projects, directed by Gregory Treverton and Michael Aho.

The research on which this volume is based was conducted at Chatham House during 1990 and the early part of 1991. It was considerably assisted by a series of study groups held at Chatham House, and I am grateful to all those, too numerous to mention by name, who contributed to these study groups from both sides of the Atlantic. Special thanks are owed to Michael Aho and Bruce Stokes from the CFR project, who provided continuous US inputs, and to officials in the Commission of the European Communities who gave much constructive advice. I am also grateful to the Council on Foreign Relations, the Institute of International Economics (Washington DC) and Centre for International Affairs (Harvard University) for facilitating round table discussions on the draft text, and to all the US participants in these groups. I would, in addition, like to thank all those people, again too numerous to list here, who took time from busy schedules to meet me or to read and comment on the draft. Needless to say I take full responsibility for the text.

The main funding for this project has been a generous grant from the Ford Foundation. The German Marshall Fund of the United States provided additional funding for US experts to take part in study groups. We are also grateful to the other funders of the European Programme of the RIIA, who have helped to make this work possible, in particular

Courtaulds, the Department of Trade and Industry, the Eurotunnel Group and the Gatsby Charitable Foundation.

Without the help of staff at Chatham House the project would not have been possible, in particular Helen Wallace for supervision and advice, Alex Bellinger and Zoë Harris for organizing study groups and preparing the text, and Margaret May for editing the final product.

October 1991   S.W.

SUMMARY

This volume looks beyond the current issues of 1992 and the Uruguay round of the GATT and aims to contribute to a better understanding of the underlying systemic factors which influence market access in the European Community and the United States. It seeks, in particular, to identify systemic differences between the two. After outlining the broad econ-omic and political background against which decisions are taken, it looks at the cases of financial services, investment, public purchasing and technical standards. In each case it makes a qualitative rather than a quantitative assessment of market access and considers policy-led efforts to enhance access at various levels – national (or EC), plurilateral (such as the OECD) and multilateral.

The GATT has been reasonably successful in reducing tariff barriers, although some still constitute important obstacles to market access, but has been much less successful at removing non-tariff barriers. During the 1970s, in the Tokyo round, it endeavoured to address non-tariff barriers resulting from the pursuit of national industrial policies by means of such instruments as subsidies or public procurement. These efforts provided a good understanding of, if not a solution to, the problems raised by this kind of non-tariff barrier, and work has continued in the Uruguay round in the 1980s.

As the 1980s progressed the focus shifted to other forms of non-tariff barrier, such as those resulting from divergent regulatory policies. These have become more important, especially in the field of services, as a result of the growing interdependence of the EC and US economies. This volume seeks to contribute to a better understanding of the impact of systemic differences in these 'new issues' areas, and of the manner in which they both affect and are affected by the current Uruguay round negotiations.

Summary

Even if the Uruguay round succeeds in dealing effectively with the existing agenda of tariffs, the older forms of non-tariff barriers and those that result from divergent regulatory policies, there is still another set of barriers to market access. These take the form of structural impediments. Most non-tariff barriers result from actions by government; in the case of structural impediments, barriers result from a *failure* of governments to act. For example, if public policy does not ensure effective competition or market transparency, other 'structural' factors may impede market access. As the industrialized economies become more integrated and other barriers are removed, such barriers assume a greater importance. They are, however, particularly difficult to deal with. Existing multilateral rules are designed to prevent governments from intervening. The US and the EC have therefore been obliged to go beyond the established multilateral rules such as *de jure* national treatment and to pursue policies based on reciprocity, equivalent competitive opportunities or *de facto* national treatment.

The study discusses three main systemic factors which could have a bearing on market access and policy in the EC and the US. First, regulatory barriers resulting from statutory measures are relatively more important in the US, where there are fewer structural impediments, than in the EC. The 1992 process is reducing or removing regulatory barriers but in so doing it is throwing the structural impediments that exist in Europe into sharper focus. Thus structural impediments are more important in the EC than in the US, but less important than in Japan.

Second, policies at the sub-federal level, and thus the relationship between the federal – or EC – level and the state level of government, have become important factors in market access. Just as domestic policies in the shape of regulatory policies became a key factor, so does state or local government regulation. Once again, there are important differences between the EC and the US. In the EC, policy integration means that the Community is assuming more and more responsibilities, especially where policies of the member states impinge upon the external economic relations of the EC. In the US, Congress seems reluctant to legislate on issues affecting the rights of the states, even when state policy is an important issue in multilateral or bilateral negotiations.

Third, just as European countries have been more prepared to intervene in order to promote national policies, so the Community is more prepared to intervene in order to create a genuine internal market, and has thus been pursuing more intrusive policies in an effort to remove structural impediments to access within the EC. This involves the exercise of supranational powers in competition policy or the introduction of common EC procedures in areas such as purchasing practices or efforts to develop common standards. Such intrusive means of opening markets are not acceptable in the US, where policies continue to be basically 'arm's-length' in nature.

The volume considers how these systemic differences feed through into policies. Since multilateral rules have a greater market-opening effect on cases in which statutory – as opposed to non-statutory – barriers to trade predominate, they will tend to open the US market more than other markets. This helps explain the more aggressive use of unilateral market-opening policies in the US, compared with the EC, and why its expectations of the Uruguay round were significantly different. The US priority in the round was to achieve concrete market-opening, as new multilateral disciplines without concrete measures would merely open the US market. More importantly, in terms of the US domestic trade policy agenda, new disciplines would tie the hands of the Congress and prevent it using unilateral instruments such as Section 301 of the US Trade Act in order to achieve concrete liberalization if the GATT fails to deliver. The EC's expectations differed in the sense that its aim was a mixture of enhanced market access, an extension of GATT rules and effective disciplining of US unilateralism.

The study concludes that the GATT in general, and a successful outcome to the Uruguay round in particular, is a necessary but not a sufficient condition for open markets. Other measures will have to be taken, both within the OECD and bilaterally, if the tensions generated by systemic differences are to be managed and contained.

Finally, it shows how the EC poses a major challenge to the US. It does so because its application of competition among rules offers an alternative approach to market liberalization to that based on the intergovernmental negotiations developed under US leadership over the past three decades. The EC also poses a challenge because of its growing weight as a trading entity, resulting from the deepening of integration through the 1992 process and the effective extension of its approach to market liberalization to include EFTA and, ultimately, the countries of Central and Eastern Europe. Systemic differences between the EC and the US will remain. This means that some trading system must be developed which can accommodate these differences. It may well be that the European Community's approach is better adapted to such a goal than that of the United States.

1
INTRODUCTION

The debate on bilateral economic relations between the European Community and the United States has focused in recent years on the external implications of 1992 and whether this represents a move towards a 'regional bloc' in Europe or even 'fortress Europe'. There has been less analysis and less discussion of market access issues in the United States and how US policy meshes with the multilateral system – in other words, of what constitutes the US, or North American, regional bloc and whether there is such a thing as 'fortress America'.

This book seeks to broaden the debate, not by producing quantitative assessments, but rather by an analysis of the more qualitative features of market access in both the EC and the US.

Definition of terms

For the purposes of the policy debate about market access in general and this book in particular it is important to be clear about what is meant by market access and a barrier to market access. A narrow definition is used in the current Uruguay round of trade negotiations in the General Agreement on Tariffs and Trade (GATT), in which a number of negotiating groups, including tariffs, non-tariff barriers, agriculture, and textiles and clothing, are collectively referred to as the 'market access issues'. A broader definition of market access, used in this book, includes all those questions being addressed in the other negotiating groups, such as services, investment, government procurement and standards. But it also includes the questions which are not in the Uruguay round such as, in particular, those raised in the Structural Impediments Initiative (SII) talks between the US and Japan.

For simplicity's sake this volume identifies four broad categories of barriers to market access: tariff barriers, two kinds of non-tariff barrier (industrial policy-related and regulatory policy-related non-tariff barriers) and structural impediments. *Tariff barriers* have been significantly reduced in a series of GATT trade negotiations over the past thirty years. They remain important in some countries, especially in middle-income or developing countries where they can be prohibitively high – up to 100 per cent. They are also important in certain sectors among industrialized countries, where tariff peaks have survived beyond liberalization.

Industrial policy-related non-tariff barriers are all those measures taken by governments that are specifically aimed at promoting the international competitiveness of an industry or company or providing protection from import competition. Such non-tariff barriers figured in the trade policy debate of the 1970s and efforts, many in vain, have been made to prohibit or at least control them in the recent GATT rounds, including the Uruguay round. Two classic examples of such non-tariff barriers are domestic subsidies and voluntary export restraint agreements.

Regulatory policy-related non-tariff barriers are those that result from national regulatory policy. In many cases trade policy, or the use of regulatory policy to promote international competitiveness or to provide protection, is not the prime objective but is the conscious or unintended by-product. The importance of divergent regulatory policies as a factor in market access grows as economies become more interdependent. Thus many of the market access issues in current trade diplomacy concern regulatory policies, such as in the field of services. As the main motivation of regulatory policies tends to be domestic policy objectives, their inclusion in international trade diplomacy means a greater degree of multilateral intrusion into domestic policy. Regulatory non-tariff barriers are in most cases also the result of positive action by government. Efforts to improve market access therefore involve the removal or modification of national regulation.

Structural impediments constitute a barrier to market access when there is an absence of effective competition or transparency in a market. The best example of how this type of barrier has entered into the policy debate is the US–Japanese SII talks, which have primarily focused on the absence of competition in a number of markets within Japan. Unlike other forms of non-tariff barrier, structural impediments are not the result of concrete action taken by governments or regulators. In some cases they may be the product of past regulatory policies, such as those which have promoted or allowed monopolistic structures, or where 'buy national' policies have promoted national champions. But in most instances they exist because of a *lack* of action by governments or the responsible authorities. When structural impediments exist, enhanced market access needs governments to take positive action, i.e. implement a more active competition policy, not simply stop doing things that create barriers. This means efforts to remove structural impediments are yet more intrusive in national policy environments.

In addition to these four types of barrier it is also helpful to distinguish between *statutory and non-statutory measures*. In many cases barriers to market access result from measures taken as a result of voluntary or corporatist decisions which have no statutory basis. For example, close links between leading companies within a sector can result in decisions to limit competition. Close links between private industry and public decision-makers can also result in covert industrial policy-related non-tariff barriers. Voluntary export restraint agreements are, for example, seldom based on any statute, but have a major impact on market access. Self-regulation such as that exercised in a number of service sectors can be the functional equivalent of statutes.

Scope of this study

The emphasis in this book is on likely future policy issues rather than on current EC–US relations. It draws on case-studies in financial services, investment, public procurement and technical standards, all areas affected by the 1992 programme. There is no case-study of agriculture, which has little to do with regulatory change as a result of 1992, although it figures, of course, in the assessment of the EC and US positions in the Uruguay round. Nor is there detailed coverage of an industrial policy case (e.g. Airbus/Boeing), which would illustrate questions of subsidies or collaborative R&D programmes.

Under US leadership, the multilateral trading system successfully reduced tariff barriers, at least between the industrialized countries, in the early GATT rounds. The Kennedy round (1962–7) and particularly the Tokyo round (1974–9) also addressed the non-tariff barriers to trade, such as subsidies, or other instruments of national industrial policy such as technical barriers to trade and government purchasing. During the 1970s work done in both the GATT and the OECD resulted in a recognition of the growing importance of these non-tariff measures designed either to promote competitiveness (e.g. subsidies) or to increase protection (e.g. quantitative restrictions), and of how they related to trade.[1] The difficulty came in deciding which subsidies should be permitted because they reflected legitimate national policy objectives, such as a balanced regional distribution of economic activity, and which should be prohibited or circumscribed because they were devised primarily to distort trade. In other words, how intrusive should multilateral rules be in denying national authorities powers to use subsidies and other equivalent measures? How much scope could there be for systemic differences in the use of such instruments without distorting trade? The Tokyo round did not produce effective means of dealing with these questions, but the issues are now broadly understood. Work on subsidies continued in the Uruguay round, which began in 1986, and which has also been the first GATT round to address regulatory barriers to trade in a serious fashion. As with subsidies the question is how intrusive multilateral rules should be in prescribing national (or EC) regulation, or alternatively how to ensure that differing regulatory systems do not result in major distortions to trade or investment.

Irrespective of the outcome of the Uruguay round, it has become clear that a similar understanding is needed concerning non-statutory regulation or 'structural impediments' to trade. Here the degree of intrusiveness of the multilateral regime assumes a different order. In the context of European integration a distinction has been made between prohibiting or removing national measures (negative integration) and taking active steps (positive integration). The analogy with the issues now being addressed in international commercial diplomacy is not quite correct, but it helps to illustrate the different nature of these issues. The question of how intrusive rules can be becomes all the more relevant when such rules seek to lay down what must be done rather than what must not be done. A further complication results from the close links between regulation and economic structure; for example, regulation of purchasing or technical standards can create supply-and-demand structures biased towards local suppliers.

In the future as in the past, therefore, the policy debate will go beyond 'trade policy' in its generally understood form and encompass domestic policy issues. The ebbing tide of tariff protection revealed first the reefs of non-tariff barriers, then the rocks of regulatory barriers and finally the diverse contours of the bedrock of structural impediments to market access.

As this coastal metaphor suggests, market access has become more and more dependent on the contours of the economic system in a country or continent. The case-studies covered are intended to contribute to a better understanding of the systemic differences that exist between the EC and the US and how they affect market access as well as the respective trade policies of these blocs. They suggest that the non-statutory structural impediments are relatively more important in the EC than in the US, where barriers are more likely to be statutory, i.e. to result from legislative actions. The cases also suggest that the 1992 process is removing many of the rocks and thus revealing some of the structural impediments that exist in Europe. As multilateral rules bear down on statutory barriers more than on non-statutory barriers, this helps to explain the disenchantment with multilateralism in the US and its more aggressive results-based trade policy, using its own national legislation and aimed at removing other countries' regulatory barriers or structural impediments in the pursuit of 'fair trade'. It also accounts for the greater urgency and higher expectations with which the US negotiated in the Uruguay round for concrete liberalization and immediate market-opening, compared with the EC and Japan; although both of these did have high expectations of the round it was rather in terms of its contribution to a general strengthening of the multilateral system.

The case-studies help to clarify other significant systemic differences between the EC and the US. Both have dualist structures, in the sense that regulatory policy is shared between the central and state authorities. With increasing economic interpenetration in both, 'sub-federal' regulation has become an important factor in market access. However, within the United States regulation is still largely determined by the principle of host state control, whereas 1992 is leading to an introduction of home country control within the EC. Community competence is on the increase in areas relevant to international negotiations, thus clarifying regulatory responsibilities; in the US the individual states continue to shape some policies, with the federal executive often unable and Congress politically reluctant to constrain them.

There are also important differences in the way regulatory barriers or structural impediments are dealt with. In order to achieve an internal market the EC has had no choice but to find a multilateral (in this case a Community) solution. As the case-studies again show, this has often taken the form of 'intrusive' EC legislation. National regulatory sovereignty has been undermined by acceptance of home country control and by mutual recognition. Where there is a legacy of structural impediments from past national regulation, such as in standards or procurement practices, the EC has pursued intrusive policies. There is also a highly intrusive supranational competition policy. But in the US the more arm's-length relationship between government and the economy means there is little support for such intrusive policies at a national level. At an international level the initial US response has been to revert to national 'unfair trade' legislation.

The case-studies show how these systemic differences have influenced the respective approaches to the multilateral trade negotiations in the GATT; while the successful conclusion of the Uruguay round is necessary, it will not be sufficient to remove the kind of barriers addressed here and which are, for better or worse, on the commercial policy agenda. The Uruguay round has three broad objectives: to extend the reach of the multilateral framework of rules, primarily to include the so-called new issues of services, trade-related investment measures (TRIMs) and trade-related intellectual property (TRIPs); to bring about concrete liberalization; and to strengthen the GATT system through enhanced transparency and stronger dispute settlement provisions.

As the Tokyo round efforts to tackle subsidies showed, drawing up rules and dispute settlement procedures will not help much when some countries use subsidies much more than others. Inevitably one country's legitimate policy instrument becomes another country's 'unfair trade' measure. The major players also disagreed about where it is legitimate for multilateral rules to 'intrude' upon national (or EC) systems.

Similar differences are to be expected over the approach to regulatory barriers and structural impediments. Within the EC the Community has developed a technique based on 'competition among rules' and supranational instruments. This is central to the 1992 programme. What is more, the EC model appears likely to be emulated in the rest of Europe through its extension to the EFTA countries and, in time, to Central and East European countries. The EC is therefore becoming a more formidable negotiating partner not only because of its economic weight but because it is internalizing an important part of the multilateral process. It is in this sense that the EC poses a systemic challenge to the US.[2] The nature of future market access issues means that this challenge goes to the heart of the national economic system. How the US responds to this challenge, and how the systemic differences are managed, will therefore have fundamental implications for transatlantic relations.

2
INTERDEPENDENCE AND POLITICAL RHETORIC

Transatlantic trade and investment relations are characterized by two contradictory trends. On the one hand there is an ever closer economic interdependence which creates a high level of policy interdependence. On the other hand there appears to be a tendency towards increasingly fractious political relations associated with claims and counter-claims about the construction of regional trading blocs. The central question for US–EC relations, therefore, is whether the two leading heavyweights of the international trading system will cooperate as trading partners or seek to score political points off each other in a way that may ultimately undermine business confidence in continued stable economic links. The US and the EC are two dominant forces in international trade. Together they account for about half of world trade, the EC 35% and the US 12%, compared with Japan's 7%. They are also still the two leading architects of the international trading system. Thus how they conduct their bilateral relations vitally affects the global trading community.

Trading partners
There is a high degree of interdependence between the EC and the US. Two-way trade was some $190bn in 1990. The EC accounts for 23% of US exports and the US for 18% of EC exports. More importantly, there is no structural deficit in transatlantic trade, whether visible or invisible

(e.g. services), as there is in the case of transpacific trade. For nearly thirty years, between 1958 and 1984, the US maintained a visible trade surplus with the EC. Unlike US–Japanese trade relations, US–EC relations are responsive to changes in macroeconomic policy and exchange rates. For example, a relatively weak dollar in the late 1970s and early 1980s resulted in a sizeable US surplus. In 1980 US exports to the EC exceeded imports by a factor of 1.74. However, this was reversed in the period 1983–6 as a result of growth induced by US fiscal expansion and a strong dollar. The US deficit with the EC grew to $20bn in 1985–6 but began to fall again as soon as relative growth in the EC picked up and after the 1985 Plaza accord among the G7 countries was successful in managing a reduction in the value of the dollar. By 1989 the US returned to a trade surplus with the EC.

Visible trade

In 1989 US exports of manufactures totalled $360bn, of which some $87bn went to the EC. Manufactures accounted for 81% of US visible exports to the EC, and agricultural products 10%. In the other direction 89% of EC exports to the US are manufactures and only 5% agricultural products. For the US the most important sectors are aircraft and aircraft parts, followed by data-processing equipment, internal combustion engines, electronics components and organic chemicals. In agriculture soya beans, other oilseeds and animal feedstuffs account for most of the US surplus with the EC.[1] In the other direction there is a somewhat wider spread of products and a bias towards beverages in the food and agricultural field. Apart from this the structure of visible trade is similar and covers a range of products.[2]

Although transatlantic trade is less characterized than transpacific trade by a concentration of exports in specific sectors, such as automobiles and electronics, the structure of trade does help to explain the respective interests in trade disputes. The weight placed on liberalization of agriculture by the US reflects the higher levels of support, especially export support, provided by the EC. Since the chief agricultural exports just listed accounted for 4–5% of US visible exports to the EC (1989 figures) it is particularly important for the US to prevent any 'rebalancing' of the Common Agricultural Policy (CAP) support programmes, which would result in increased import protection or tariffs on its principal products. The US preoccupation with launch aid or exchange-rate guarantees for Airbus is also understandable given that the airframe industry accounted for no less than 8% of US exports to the EC throughout the second half of the 1980s.

In general terms the EC's trade with the US is broadly based. There are no cases in which trade in one sector is so important that it has a disproportionate impact on the EC's policy vis-à-vis the US. The size and significance of the US market means it is important to virtually all sectors of industry within the EC. This may help to explain why the EC interest in trade negotiations (see below) has primarily been in more horizontal issues such as ensuring that US trade remedies are subject to GATT discipline.

Services

Transatlantic interdependence is even higher in services, where US exports totalled $110bn in 1989, of which nearly one-third, or $33bn, went to the EC. The US has an overall surplus in services of about $30bn but is in a broad balance of trade in services with the EC ($106m deficit for the US in 1989).[3] The US interest in liberalizing trade in services clearly stems from the country's sizeable surplus in this sector, compared with its persistent deficit in manufactures. In 1989 it had a surplus of $0.5bn in business services related to information technology, which also helps to explain its interest in a general liberalization of (tele)comm-unications. The US interest in intellectual property reflects its worldwide $9bn surplus from royalties, of which revenue from the EC accounts for half. Likewise the dispute over the EC's broadcasting directive, which set a high ceiling on US sales of motion pictures and television pro-grammes to Europe, touches on the interests of a sector in which the US had a surplus of nearly $0.8bn in 1989 and in which there is a highly influential domestic lobby.

Equally, the EC's support for the negotiation of a General Agreement on Trade in Services (GATS) is consistent with its surplus in services, including with the US. For the EC the strongest service sector is travel (expenditure by visitors): it had a surplus of $2bn with the US in 1989. There is also a surplus ($2.2bn in 1989) with the US in insurance premium receipts, most of which most go to British firms. This may help to explain the EC's interest in ensuring that financial services form part of the GATS and not a separate agreement (see Chapter 3).

In telecommunications services the US runs a deficit with the EC ($0.7bn in 1989), as with most other countries, owing to the fact that international charges are lower in the US than in the more regulated EC telecommunications services, so that there are more outgoing calls from the US than vice versa.

9

Investment

Interdependence is also reflected in increased foreign direct investment (FDI). By 1990 some 38% of the stock of US foreign investment was in the EC, up from 18% in 1960. Moreover, US investment in the EC shows a relatively higher rate of return. It currently accounts for over half the revenue from US foreign direct investment.[4] The flow of new FDI is more variable, but over the period 1985–9 some 40% of US foreign investment went into the EC. In the other direction no less than 58% of the total FDI stock in the US is of EC origin (65% from EC plus EFTA), and over the period 1985–9 the EC has supplied 60% of the inflow of FDI into the US.

No less than 83% of the income from foreign direct investment in the US went to EC-based companies. In 1989 foreign companies bought assets in the US totalling $64bn. EC-based companies accounted for a little under half of this ($31.6bn), of which British companies alone spent no less than $23bn. In the other direction there has also been a marked increase in US acquisition activity in Europe, again notably in Britain. The increase in US investment in the EC has been attributed, in part, to the desire of US firms to establish a presence in the EC in the run-up to the internal market in 1992, but the fact that there is as much investment flowing in the other direction suggests that a general process of internationalization is under way.[5] Major companies seek to ensure they have a presence in each market. Thus increased investment in the EC, whether in the form of greenfield investment or acquisitions, must be seen against this global background.

The internationalization of the production and supply of goods and services is also reflected in the figures for the sales of foreign affiliates. In 1988 the sales of the EC affiliates of US companies amounted to no less than $600bn.[6] The same companies employed 2.6 million people in the EC. US affiliates of EC-owned companies totalled sales of $400bn in 1988 and employed 2 million people.[7]

The effects of interdependence

The picture that emerges is of a high degree of transatlantic economic interdependence and industrial interpenetration, in which the policy decisions taken by either the US or the EC, or by other actors such as Japan, have an immediate effect – both negative and positive – on their trading partners. Policy interdependence can result in a negative dynamic when protectionist measures taken by one country are followed by others in an effort to prevent or anticipate trade diversion, as is shown by the history of import restrictions in textiles and clothing. The US decision to control cotton textiles in the early 1960s was followed by the EC. The Europeans then sought to extend coverage to other fibres as well in order to prevent exporters replacing cotton with man-made fibre products. The US then followed suit in order to prevent trade diversion, and the Multi-Fibre Arrangement came into being. There have been similar examples in the steel industry at the end of the 1970s and car imports from Japan in the early 1980s.

There has also been a good deal of imitation of national trade legislation, especially in the field of 'instruments of commercial defence'. The EC and the US have imitated each other's anti-dumping legislation. The EC's New Commercial Instrument (NCI), introduced in 1985 to deal with 'unfair' trade practices, was modelled on Section 301 of the US Trade Act of 1974 (later revised in the 1980 Trade Agreements Act and the 1988 Omnibus Trade and Competitiveness Act).

More recently, the US and the EC have both introduced forms of 'reciprocity'. The evolution of the concept of reciprocity owes much to the work of the US Congress, in the early 1980s. As is the practice in Congress, radical bills (draft legislation) were introduced with little prospect of adoption. But these laid the foundations for the ultimately more balanced measures introduced in the 1988 Omnibus Trade Act.[8] European countries also made use of the concept in national statutes, most notably in provisions concerning market access in financial services markets. Paradoxically it was the liberal-minded Thatcher government in Britain that provided the European model for reciprocity in the 1985 Financial Services Act (FSA). This model was then used in the EC's Second Banking Coordination Directive (SBCD), which was in turn used as the model for the US Fair Trade in Financial Services Act of 1990 (see Chapter 3).

Policy interdependence need not always create a protectionist dynamic. Within the EC, the high degree of economic interdependence has also created pressure for policy harmonization. In the 1992 programme this has been channelled to positive ends by the establishment of a statutory framework for competition among rules. Faced with an ever-increasing level of economic interdependence and the difficulty of harmonizing regulatory policies across its member states, the Community has increasingly shifted to an approach based on mutual recognition of national standards and home state regulatory control. With this approach the operations of companies in host states are based on home state regulation. There is therefore no incentive for individual states to pursue restrictive policies because these would simply place their national companies at a disadvantage. Or again, higher corporation tax in one member state adversely affects the competitive position of companies based in that state. This is accentuated when, under the EC policy of home country control, companies paying the lower taxes can supply goods or services throughout the EC. In the case of the EC, policy interdependence has therefore created a pressure for deregulation.[9]

Similar pressures operate internationally. To a greater or lesser degree a form of *de facto* competition among rules operates internationally and especially in certain areas of EC–US relations. As the case-studies in the following chapters will show, this is what occurs in banking, where free capital movement is creating the kind of conditions in which competition among the various regulatory regimes is increasing the pressure for convergence. Thus market forces can bring about a convergence which will facilitate trade and investment and minimize disputes, but market forces are not enough. For such a process to operate, policy must provide a framework which makes increased market integration credible. In recent years the political rhetoric has been working against such an objective by inflating relatively minor trade disputes and giving credence to the perception that the process under way is leading to the creation of regional trading blocs rather than further international economic integration.

Trading blows

Transatlantic trade relations have never been free from tension. At regular intervals there have been significant disputes, some of which have threatened to escalate into major trade wars. In most cases these have affected relatively insignificant volumes of trade. During the 1960s there was the so-called chicken war. More seriously, during the early 1980s there were a number of disputes resulting from systemic differences over non-tariff barriers such as national subsidies. A case in point was the steel industry, in which divergent approaches to dealing with global surplus capacity created serious transatlantic trade frictions.[10] Similar systemic differences resulted in trade tensions with Japan, which was accused of using 'unfair' means of targeting specific industries such as steel and, later, cars and thus helping to create the surplus capacity in the first place.

More recently there was the 1988–9 hormone dispute, caused when the EC introduced legislation banning the use of growth-generating hormones. This affected US exports to the EC, which accounted for less than 0.1% of trade; on occasions, however, the heated political rhetoric suggested that the dispute could escalate into a damaging trade war.

At the same time the political tensions began to centre on the perception in certain sections of the US policy community that the EC's internal market programme was contributing to the construction of a 'fortress Europe'. The EC responded in 1989 by intensifying its attack on what was broadly perceived in Europe as a drift towards unilateralism in US trade policy. Just as these tensions began to subside the transatlantic war of words over the Uruguay round began, with the US accusing the EC of becoming 'inward-looking' and jeopardizing the whole round by refusing to negotiate on agriculture.

Fortress Europe

The EC's 1992 programme began to gain momentum in the summer of 1987, attracting broad public attention in late 1987 or early 1988. During the summer of 1988 there was much talk about the single or internal market and conferences on the subject proliferated, leading to a widespread awareness of 'EC–92' in the US. Until this time the US trade policy community, in the shape of Congress, the responsible administration officials and above all the Washington lawyers serving Congress and the business lobbies, was preoccupied with the Omnibus Trade and Competitiveness Act and the US–Canada Free Trade Agreement. US businesses with an existing presence in Europe (the 'insiders') had, of course, been aware of what was going on from an early stage in the 1992 programme; they were generally multinational companies with a presence across the whole of the EC. Such companies were well placed to benefit from the removal of barriers to trade within the Community and supported the 1992 programme because it promised faster growth and reduced costs for their European operations. It was the 'outsiders', the US companies without operations in Europe, that were most worried by the 1992 programme when they first became aware of it in late 1988.

The US political debate on 1992 was precipitated by a number of insiders playing the fortress Europe card as a means of galvanizing support for their efforts to influence EC directives. The main target of this lobbying effort was the European Commission's draft of the Second Banking Coordination Directive. This contained very general provisions on 'reciprocity'. A number of (non-bank) US financial service companies, such as American Express, viewed this with considerable concern. They had just concluded a successful fight against 'protectionist',

13

'mirror-image' reciprocity in the US Congress, and feared that if the wording on reciprocity in the Commission's proposal remained vague, it would open the way for the EC to pursue just such a policy.

In July and August 1988 External Affairs Commissioner Willy de Clerq made a number of speeches in which he stressed that foreign firms would not automatically benefit from the market-liberalizing measures of 1992, if their home markets did not provide equivalent access for EC-based companies. The insider lobbies picked up the idea of fortress Europe as a means of gaining the attention of the US policy community. The initial response of Congress was that the administration had, once again, been failing to look after US interests.[11] The outsiders became alarmed. With little knowledge of the workings of the EC or the 1992 programme, the basic assumption soon gained hold that the Europeans would shift the inevitable costs of internal liberalization on to third countries. The issue of whether 1992 represented a generalized threat of fortress Europe then rapidly became the main trade policy issue in Washington. The Europeans were caught off-guard. In 1988 no systematic thought had been given to the political impact of the 1992 programme on the EC's trading partners, and the Commission and member states were obliged to rectify this rapidly, by producing a declaration on its external implications.[12]

The fortress Europe debate was driven by a number of factors. Not only companies wishing to influence EC directives found it helpful to attract the attention of policy-makers in the US. Other lobbies, already engaged in trade disputes with the EC (such as the exporters of beef in the hormone case) also found it useful to play the fortress Europe card and to do so more publicly, in order to bring pressure to bear on the EC. Unlike the US multinationals, which already had a presence in the EC, such companies did not take into account the fact that they would, in general, benefit from the 1992 process. In this way lobbies that had for some time been seeking better access to the EC market, such as providers of telecommunications equipment or services, or the power plant industry, took advantage of the fortress Europe idea (see Box 2.1).

The introduction of new EC-level directives or regulations which discriminated against the US also helped inflame the fortress Europe debate. For many years the supporters of liberal trade in Washington had argued for unqualified national treatment as the basis for US commercial policy. National treatment means that any imported product, once in the national market, should be given the same treatment as a local product. The liberal trade lobby in the US had made good use of unqualified

Box 2.1 Telecommunications and fortress Europe

Telecommunications provides a good example of how the fortress Europe idea figured in the US domestic political debate. During the 1980s the US had deregulated its telecommunications sector. This was done largely through the courts rather than Congress, and little thought was given to the external trade implications. Deregulation resulted in a unilateral opening of the US market and the loss of market access as a lever to open export markets for US suppliers.[13] Subsequently the US industry has worked to make good what it lost in the early 1980s. It has sponsored trade legislation based on sectoral reciprocity, which would enable access to the US telecommunications market to be restricted if foreign countries fail to open their markets to US suppliers.

After a number of attempts to introduce such legislation in the mid-1980s, the industry finally succeeded in getting a reciprocity provision in the 1988 Trade and Competitiveness Act empowering the administration to restrict imports of telecommunications equipment into the US in such cases.[14] Congress supported such a measure because it gave back some leverage to US negotiators within the GATT or bilateral discussions. But the administration was reluctant to implement the Act's provisions, especially against the EC, for fear of precipitating retaliation and major trade tensions. By fanning the flames of the fortress Europe debate within the US political community, the domestic lobby could bring pressure on the administration to act more aggressively. Under the provisions of the 1988 Act it was first necessary for the EC to be identified as pursuing 'unfair' trade practices in telecommunications. The Community was identified in 1989, with respect to German purchasing practices in particular. In 1990 the US administration postponed any action against the EC until the conclusion of the Uruguay round.

national treatment in order to oppose US protectionist legislation seeking to discriminate against foreign suppliers. Within the EC, Article 58 (EEC) provides an effective guarantee of national treatment for any company, regardless of origin.

In a number of areas both the EC and the US have in practice qualified the concept of national treatment. As both seek to ensure equivalent competitive opportunities, it is no longer *de jure* but *de facto* national treatment that counts. Within the EC, there was a strongly argued case that the Community was offering greater access to its own market than its competitors were, as a result of the 1992 programme, with its mutual recognition and active efforts to open markets combined with the existence of Article 58 (EEC). Consequently reciprocity or third-country provisions (discussed in the case-studies below) were added to some key directives. Such qualification of national treatment, as in the SBCD or the utilities directive in public procurement, was regarded by the Washington trade lawyers as fundamentally wrong and as the first step down a slippery slope to protectionism. The fact that US trade policy in a number of areas was also straying beyond *de jure* national treatment into *de facto* national treatment was conveniently ignored or justified on the grounds that it was seeking to prise open closed markets, not close the US market.

In many ways it was the visibility of the discrimination against the US that was most important. One of the effects of the 1992 programme of legislation has been a shift towards the use of EC statutory provisions and away from the use of discretionary powers by national authorities. The transparency of such measures meant they could be more easily attacked than the covert and generally more protectionist national measures they replaced. This shift towards statutory barriers to trade represents a convergence between the EC and US, because the US system (see below) is also based on legislation rather than on discretion.

In the second half of 1988 a number of investigations and inter-agency reports and groups set to work analysing the impact of 1992 on the US. Possibly the most comprehensive of these was the International Trade Commission's report of July 1989.[15] This argued that 1992 would, on balance, mean a more open European market and would thus be beneficial for the US. By mid-1990 a consensus had been established that 1992 would not result in a fortress Europe, but that it was important to keep a close watch on specific parts of the programme, such as standards, public procurement and investment policy.[16]

US unilateralism

Faced with the US challenge on fortress Europe, the EC responded in kind. There had long been concern, both in Europe and elsewhere, about the growing use of 'unilateralist' methods of trade liberalization based on US domestic trade legislation. The EC challenged the inclusion of reciprocity provisions in the 1988 US Trade Act, arguing that they were not GATT conform. This held not only for the Gephardt amendment, which would have required the US administration to act when there was a structural imbalance in trade with any country, but also for the less blatantly unilateralist use of US trade legislation, such as Super 301 or indeed Section 301 itself.

Section 301 of the 1974 Trade Act provides for remedies against cases of 'unfair trade'. Critics of this general provision argue that it allows the US to determine unilaterally what is and what is not 'fair trade', whereas such decisions should be taken within a multilateral framework. For its part the US argues that on the whole Section 301 merely enables Congress to ensure that the administration is apprised of 'unfair' policies and practices. On the rare occasions when action is taken against imports into the US it is only because there is no adequate multilateral provision, because the practice in question is not yet covered by the GATT, or because the country concerned has not respected or has frustrated GATT rules. US liberal traders have also argued that Super 301 was the least of the evils and the best that could be achieved, meaning the least unilateralist, given the mood in Congress at the time. Super 301 required the administration to produce comprehensive reports on barriers to trade. Once a barrier based on 'unfair' practice or policy had been identified, there was then an obligation on the administration do something about it or to explain why this was not in the national interest.[17] Super 301 ran for only two years, 1989 and 1990, but the general powers under Section 301 remain, as do specific powers in certain sectors, discussed in the case-studies below.

In May 1989 the US administration announced which policies and practices it would seek to have removed under the Super 301 provisions. The EC used this as a stick with which to beat the US in the mutual recriminations about trade policy. Not to be outdone by the US reports listing barriers to trade, the European Commission introduced its own list of US 'unfair' trade barriers, and has subsequently published it each year at about the same time as the *Report on Barriers to Trade* produced by the US Trade Representative's office.[18] At the OECD ministerial meeting in May 1989 the EC orchestrated an attack on the US, accusing it of undermining the multilateral trading system. As in the US, EC lobbies seeking protection for themselves stressed the unilateral interpretation of fair trade by the US and argued that the EC should do the same. Many industrial interests lament the fact that the EC has no effective equivalent to Section 301.

The Uruguay round

The Uruguay round provides another example of the use of political rhetoric in trade diplomacy. It is not possible here to provide a detailed account of the political, let alone the technical, issues in all fifteen of the negotiating groups of the round.[19] Each of the case-studies in the following chapters deals with the relevant negotiating groups in some detail, but some discussion of the round as a whole and agriculture in particular is necessary to understand the recent history of EC–US trade relations.

The predominant public perception in the US was that the EC was foot-dragging on the Uruguay round negotiations. This view was not

17

held by negotiators nor indeed by those close to the negotiations, who had a more nuanced understanding, but by Congress and some people in the private sector, and had originated at a time when the EC was less enthusiastic on a number of negotiating groups.[20] For example, the EC originally sided with the developing countries in seeking to limit the negotiations on intellectual property – a high-priority topic for the US – so that they covered copyright only and not patents. The EC position changed after 1986, once the negotiations were under way and after important European companies had been recruited into a US-led international business coalition promoting tougher protection of intellectual property rights. The EC subsequently became a strong supporter of the TRIPs negotiations. Likewise on TRIMs, the EC objectives in the negotiations were more modest than those of the US, focusing on a narrow range of investment performance requirements.[21]

But the 'foot-dragging' perception was heightened later by the EC's apparent preoccupation with developments within Europe, such as the 1992 programme, the negotiations with EFTA on a European Economic Area, German unification and revolutionary change in Central and Eastern Europe. During 1990 the addition of the two Intergovernmental Conferences (on economic and monetary union and on political union) was seen as further proof of Eurocentricity. This was epitomized for many Americans by the Community's decision, at the informal Rome European Council in October 1990, to move ahead with economic and monetary union but its failure, at the same meeting, to take any decision on its position on agriculture in the Uruguay round.

Agriculture
Agriculture was, of course, a key area.[22] In previous GATT rounds too the US had started with ambitious plans. In the Kennedy round agreement had been close on measures that would have imposed controls on the level of support provided for agriculture, but EC defence of the CAP meant that these failed to meet US expectations and the round was concluded without agreement on a general limitation of support. Likewise in the Tokyo round US ambitions ran headlong into the EC's defence of the CAP. Faced with a choice of agreement on a package for the round without agriculture or no agreement at all, the US administration opted for the latter. A political compromise was found for export subsidies, based on wording which urged Contracting Parties of the GATT to avoid using them to take more than their traditional share of export markets. This compromise failed to work effectively because of

fierce competition between EC and US exporters, both of whom benefited from export support. The absence of any agreement meant there was still no multilateral discipline on agricultural subsidies during the 1980s. The lesson the EC agricultural lobbies drew from these previous attempts was that if one waited long enough the US would be forced to cave in, or at least to moderate its position.

In the Uruguay round the US again began by setting what were in European eyes hopelessly ambitious targets for reductions in the level of subsidy – even their complete elimination. The Reagan administration was more or less obliged to pursue such a line because it had argued, during the mid-1980s, that the malaise of US farming and the growing trade deficit could be resolved if the Uruguay round allowed better access for US farm exports in foreign markets. The US also started the round determined that this time it would not capitulate, and its negotiators repeatedly stated that no agreement was better than a bad agreement.[23]

The first crisis over agriculture occurred at the mid-term review meeting, held in Montreal in December 1988. The US, supported by the Cairns group,* pressed for agreement on the basis of the elimination of agricultural subsidies. The EC rejected this as unrealistic and the result was deadlock. At a second attempt, in Geneva in March 1989, it was agreed that the negotiations should aim for a 'substantial and progressive reduction' of agricultural support 'over a specified period of time'.[24] This was generally interpreted in the EC as meaning that the US was at last prepared to accept reasonable objectives and give up the idea of elimination. But the US position paper on agriculture, submitted in the autumn of 1989, reverted to elimination as an objective, albeit over a phased period of five years for export and ten for domestic subsidies.

Throughout 1989 the EC sought to avoid negotiating on agriculture and to deflect the political campaign against its agricultural policies by pointing to the protectionist pressures in textiles in the US. Both sides battled to shape the agendas for the quadripartite meetings of trade ministers from the US, the EC, Japan and Canada. The EC tried to ensure that Section 301 and textiles were top of the agenda, while the US insisted on agriculture as a priority. During this period the agricultural lobbies in the EC were of the opinion that the Community should 'tough it out' in the expectation that the US, under pressure from its own farming lobbies, would ultimately be forced to make concessions. Faced

*Argentina, Australia, Brazil, Canada, Chile, Colombia, Hungary, Indonesia, Malaysia, New Zealand, Thailand, Uruguay.

with this intransigence, the US negotiators carried the debate into the public arena. Although this was perhaps unavoidable it reduced the scope for compromise. Having publicly attacked the EC's unwillingness to negotiate, the US administration could not easily reach accommodation without being accused by an ever more sceptical Congress that it was turning soft on the foreigners.

A second crisis occurred at the Houston summit of July 1990. Again the US launched a public attack on the EC, but wording was found giving support for the approach proposed by the chairman of the GATT negotiating group on agriculture, a senior official in the Dutch ministry of agriculture, Mr de Zeeuw. The key issue by this stage of the talks was whether there should be a commitment to specific reductions in each of the three areas of negotiation: export subsidies, domestic subsidies and transforming import restrictions into tariffs (as the first stage of a liberalization process in which the tariffs would be progressively negotiated away). The EC favoured an approach in which each Contracting Party of the GATT would agree to reduce support by a set amount. For this purpose all forms of support would be cumulated in an Aggregate Measure of Support (AMS), which would allow support for different types of agricultural product to be 'rebalanced'. The main area of interest was soya beans and oilseeds: the EC farm lobby had for some years wished to see changes that would enable the Community to raise its low or zero-bound tariffs in order to protect this sector, but also as a means of raising revenue. But naturally the US government wished at all costs to avoid rebalancing these key sectors. More generally, the US and the Cairns group wanted specific commitments on reductions in support in each category. The de Zeeuw text sought a compromise by incorporating the principle of AMS and tariffication, but also called for export subsidies to be reduced by more than domestic subsidies. This was supported by everyone except the EC.

The Brussels ministerial meeting
Shortly after Houston, in July 1990, the Trade Negotiations Committee (TNC), the high-level coordinating committee for the round, met in Geneva to agree on the timetable for the last phase of the negotiations leading up to the ministerial meeting in Brussels in early December 1990. Negotiating positions had to be submitted by 13 October 1990. These were to specify the existing levels of support and the level of reductions in support each Contracting Party was prepared to offer. At the end of July Ray McSharry, the EC Commissioner responsible for

agriculture, proposed a 30% reduction on an AMS basis. This meant that the EC would be able to increase the level of support for certain products provided there was an overall reduction of 30%. This was rejected by the US and the Cairns Group, but proved to be still too great a reduction for the European farm lobbies and for a majority of the member states. Despite marathon meetings of the Council of Ministers – both agriculture ministers and foreign ministers as well as 'jumbo councils' consisting of both – the EC was unable to present a negotiating position on time.

What finally emerged on 7 November was not substantially different from the initial Commission proposal. At this stage there was not much time left to negotiate, and in any case the difficulty in reaching an agreement meant that the Commission had little if any negotiating flexibility. Clearly the agricultural interests in the EC were still pursuing a strategy of 'toughing it out'. Nevertheless the Commission did move to make a concession during the Brussels ministerial meeting. It offered to accept the condition sought by the US and the Cairns group that there should be negotiations on specific commitments in each of the three areas of export and domestic support and import restrictions/tariffication. The US administration was not prepared to accept this offer and the talks came to an end in Brussels when a number of disgruntled Latin American countries walked out. In order to keep the round going, and in particular to enable the US administration to argue in Congress for an extension of its negotiating authority for the round, the so-called Dunkel text, named after the Secretary-General of the GATT, was agreed on 28 February 1991 in Geneva. This text contained more or less what had been offered by the Commission in Brussels, namely that the EC was prepared to enter into binding negotiations on the three forms of support. The Dunkel text allowed technical negotiations to continue in Geneva pending the extension of the fast-track procedure by the US Congress and a political understanding on the nature of the final package of agreements for the round.

Had it not been for differences over agriculture the prospects for a positive outcome from the Brussels meeting would have been much higher. On the rest of the fifteen negotiating groups there had been significant progress, which was continued in Brussels. Furthermore, agriculture was the only issue on which the EC was alone in holding up progress. In other areas, such as services, textiles and possibly tariffs, it was the US that was in an isolated position: in services because of its opposition to most favoured nation (mfn) coverage of service sectors (see Chapter 3); in textiles because of the administration's difficulty in containing the domestic pressure for continued protection; and in tariffs because the US was virtually alone in holding out against a systematic formula approach to further tariff reductions. On many issues, such as intellectual property, dispute settlement, TRIMs and rules of origin, the EC and the US were in broad agreement. In some areas both were happier to make less progress, for instance over anti-dumping, on which Japan and Hong Kong were very keen to see more GATT discipline. In reality, therefore, the picture was highly complex, as was only to be expected with 106 countries and fifteen negotiating groups. But for the domestic political audience, representatives of the US administration and private sector placed the blame squarely on the EC. As a result the general perception in US policy circles is that the EC is wholly responsible for the failure of the Brussels meeting.

In this sense there can be little doubt that the EC's handling of the agricultural issue represents a significant diplomatic and political defeat for the Community. But there were two underlying reasons for the failure in Brussels: first, the differing expectations of the major Contracting Parties, and second, the failure of trade diplomacy to find a package that all negotiators could sell to their domestic political constituencies.

Expectations of the Uruguay round

Expectations in the US Congress and business circles about the Uruguay round had been high. As is often the case in US trade policy, the administration argued that progress had to be made if Congress was to be satisfied. It was also argued that the demands of key private sector interests, such as those seeking tougher GATT protection for intellectual property rights or enhanced market access for US service exports, would have to be met because their support was essential if Congress was to agree on the final package. The administration used the now well-worn argument that if it could not get a respectable agreement it could not contain protectionist pressures in Congress. But the general drift towards unilateralism in US trade policy means that these domestic pressures can never be satisfied. US negotiators argued that, far from the US having set its sights too high, the others, especially the EC and Japan, had set theirs too low.[25]

The key issue, as will be shown below, is not the level but the kind of expectation. The US domestic constituency, in the shape of Congress and the private lobbies, expected the US administration to deliver immediate market liberalization – in other words, a rapid return on the political capital invested in the negotiations. By the end of 1990 what counted in terms of 'selling the results back home' was thus not necessarily more multilateralism but more dollars in the cash registers of US exporters.[26] The EC (and Japanese) expectations were more balanced in the sense that a result that would contribute to strengthening and extending the GATT was seen as worthwhile in its own right, regardless of the degree of concrete market-opening – though of course enhanced market access was important.

The EC also expects to get a stronger set of GATT rules and an agreement that all Contracting Parties will feel it is to their advantage to sign. After some initial hesitation the EC strongly supported extending the GATT to include services, TRIPs and TRIMs. Its support for more effective rule-making in the GATT was also reflected in its significant shift towards accepting more adjudication than negotiation in GATT dispute settlement. Thus it supported the enhanced dispute settlement provisions negotiated in the round even though they meant an end to the existing practice of unanimity in the adoption of panel reports. In other words, the internal political pressures on EC negotiators were less intense than in the US. There was no domestic constituency ready and willing to vote down an agreement because the results were not concrete enough in terms of immediate improvements in market access.

The negotiating mandate agreed in 1986 which formed the basis of the EC's position throughout the round also had a hidden agenda: to contain the growth of US unilateralism. The EC mandated its negotiators to find means of dealing with the 'maintenance by certain Contracting Parties of national legislation, or even the enactment of new legislation [such as the 1988 US Trade Act] which is in clear breach of GATT obligations'. It also called for a review of the benefits accruing to federal states by virtue of the non-application of certain GATT provisions at the sub-federal level. The mandate shows that the EC was already aware of US expectations and warned that 'the trading community [would be] badly served by over-ambitious programmes accompanied by unrealistic expectations'.

The failure of trade diplomacy
The fact that the negotiations were carried out in an acrimonious public contest made the task of trade diplomacy harder. At the close of the Tokyo round it had still been possible for the key negotiators, including those from the EC and the US, to find an accommodation that each could sell to the domestic constituency. This was not possible at the Brussels meeting for a number of reasons, including the complexity of the negotiations and the personalities involved. In addition, the general atmosphere of confrontation rather than cooperation that existed within the

domestic constituencies meant that it was hard for either side to make concessions without seeming weak.

When it came to it there was no incentive for the US administration to make concessions in Brussels, least of all on agriculture. First, it could not afford to risk a compromise only to have Congress subsequently vote against implementing legislation. Had this happened the US would have been blamed for undermining the multilateral trading system. Second, a concession on agriculture would have exposed the US on a number of other negotiating groups where it rather than the EC was holding back agreement. By far the best strategy for the US administration therefore was also to 'hang tough' on agriculture; if the negotiations were to fail it was better that this should happen in Brussels and for the EC to take the blame. That is why the EC's inability to produce a reasonable position on agriculture was such a diplomatic failure.

Regional trading blocs
There has been a packed European agenda in the period since 1987, leading to a widespread perception that the EC was in some way inward-looking. There was considerable concern in some countries, such as Japan, that the trend was towards the creation of regional trading blocs. American concern, however, was tempered by the fact that the US was entering into regional negotiations of its own, in the shape of the North American Free Trade Agreement (NAFTA), which included Canada and Mexico.

Figures showing a relative growth in intra-regional trade have been used to support the view that such blocs were being created. There is little doubt that intra-regional trade is important. Western Europe as a whole (EC plus EFTA) accounts for 44% of world trade; as much as two-thirds of this (West) European trade is intra-regional. But in North America (i.e. the US, Canada and Mexico) the proportion is reversed: only one-third of trade is intra-regional. Taking a longer-term perspective, both intra-EC and extra-EC trade developed at more or less the same rate from the creation of the EC until 1984. Extra-EC trade grew faster during the mid-1960s, mid-1970s and early 1980s; intra-EC trade grew faster in 1970–4, 1977–9, and 1981–4.[27] Intra-EC trade accounted for about half of EC trade from 1960 until the mid-1980s. But in 1984, at a time when extra-EC imports were declining as a result of falling oil and raw materials prices, intra-EC trade climbed to 58%, subsequently remaining at this level. EC exports to the US also declined more during this period than did intra-EC trade; in any event, the fall in exports to the US occurred before the introduction of the 1992 programme and certainly before the idea of a single market had gained any momentum.

It is also important to recall the differences between these supposed regional blocs. The EC has a customs union and a common commercial policy. There are supranational institutions and Community law is binding over the jurisdictions of nation-states. Efforts are even now under way to establish a common currency. The NAFTA constitutes a free trade agreement, not a customs union. The participating countries have no common commercial policy, no supranational institutions and no directly applicable supranational law. Finally, the so-called East Asian 'bloc' consists of little more than a group of countries with close trading relations. And yet by 1990 it had become almost an article of faith that such blocs were in the making. The problem with such incautious use of political rhetoric is that it is all too readily seized on by protectionist lobbies as a means of justifying their own positions.

Conclusions

Transatlantic trade and investment relations operate on two planes, political and corporate. On the corporate plane trade and above all investment continue to grow, with the result that economic interdependence increases. Where there are local market conditions or regulatory measures which require companies to adapt they do so. For example, a European bank wishing to enter the US retail banking sector adapts to US state and federal regulations, even if this means it cannot offer the same kind of services as it does in Europe. Equally if a US company, for reasons of corporate strategy, wishes to have a presence in the EC it will accept the prevailing rules of the game and operate within them. Through investment multinational companies can therefore get round many of the regulatory and structural barriers to market access. As will be shown in later chapters, there are no significant barriers to transatlantic investment. There are certain prescribed areas, such as shipping and broadcasting, where improvements could be made, and structural impediments also exist in the shape of monopolies, but this does not change the general position that most multinational companies can, and do, do business across the Atlantic with little difficulty. There is no structural imbalance in transatlantic trade, as there is, for example, in transpacific trade. If trade gaps develop it is because of movements in exchange rates or relative rates of growth. All this suggests that the EC and the US will remain trading partners.

The political plane, by contrast, is characterized by some shrill language and mutual recrimination. The two heavyweights of international trade seem at times more than ready to stand and trade blows. The interaction between the political and corporate planes will therefore determine EC–US trade relations. The following chapters provide some examples of this interaction.

3
FINANCIAL SERVICES

The financial services sector provides some valuable insights into how structural and regulatory barriers affect market access. The progressive liberalization of international capital movements, and enhanced communications technology allowing 24-hour financial market operation, have resulted in increased interdependence in banking and other financial services and a globalization of markets. Such recent developments as Europe's 1992 programme and the US debate on regulatory reform of financial services can be seen as policy responses to this globalization.

The 1992 process is bringing about dynamic change in European financial services and reducing or removing statutory barriers to market access, and has precipitated significant corporate restructuring in the shape of mergers and acquisitions and an increase in cross-shareholdings and joint ventures. Even after 1993 access to parts of the EC market, such as retail financial services, will require local presence. By hastening consolidation and restructuring of the European market, the 1992 programme is making strategic acquisitions by non-EC companies harder. The removal of statutory barriers in the shape of regulation will throw into focus such structural impediments.

In the US change is less dynamic because reform is inhibited by long-established state rights to regulate and the exercise of host state regulatory control. As a result statutory barriers will remain the focus of the policy debate in the US, especially at the state level. This difference could become a source of tension in EC–US relations. In trade policy terms the EC will be interested in ensuring that multilateral discipline bears down on US statutory barriers, at both federal and state levels. For the US the emphasis will be on developing means of dealing with structural impediments. This difference of interest is illustrated in the respective EC and US approaches to the GATS negotiations in the Uruguay round. On the positive side of the equation the global nature of money markets, combined with the close links between regulatory authorities in financial services in various countries, is creating a kind of *de facto* competition among rules which may well be more effective in opening markets than either multilateral or bilateral trade diplomacy.

The structure of the sector

The financial services sector consists of three main sectors, banking, securities and insurance.[1] Each is in turn made up of different sub-sectors, which exhibit differing degrees of internationalization.

Banking can be roughly divided into wholesale (or investment) banking, in which services are provided predominantly to large corporate customers, and retail banking for smaller businesses or individuals. There is already considerable international competition in wholesale banking although market barriers still remain. For example, the Bank for International Settlements (BIS) estimates that the stock of international financing, which is used as a proxy for international banking activity, increased from $1,500bn in 1983 to $3,200 bn in 1988.[2] On the other hand, markets for retail banking remain local. For example, a Bavarian farmer will not generally hold his current account in Paris, nor insure his tractor in London.[3] At the moment retail banking and insurance are still effectively closed to cross-border competition, and market access will, in practice, still require the establishment of a local subsidiary. This applies to both the EC and the US, at least in the short to medium term.

The international *securities* business has also increased in recent years. There has been a growing securitization of financial markets, with a larger share of funding for companies taking the form of securities (or equity rather than bank lending). This international business has tended to be drawn towards the larger capital markets such as London, New York and Tokyo. The average market capitalization as a percentage of GNP is one indicator of the size of these markets: it is 92% in Japan, 80% in the UK and 58% in the US, compared with only 21% in Germany and 18% in France.[4] The number of companies listed on the larger markets is also greater – about 2,000 in Tokyo and London and 7,000 in the United States, compared with about 500 in France and Germany. In Europe trading in securities is carried out by either merchant banks or universal banks which provide a range of services, including deposit-taking. In the US and Japan regulation still separates banking and securities.

The *insurance* sector also consists of different elements. Non-life insurance roughly mirrors investment banking and life insurance mirrors retail banking, but there are trends towards more cross-border trade, especially in the shape of reinsurance and life insurance (or mass risks). Here, as in retail banking, there has been very little cross-border supply of services, and suppliers generally need a local presence in order to gain effective access to the market. The insurance market is larger in the US than in the EC, accounting for 38% of world insurance premiums ($406bn) in 1987, as against about 25% for the EC. This is due to the relatively underdeveloped markets in southern member states of the Community, especially in life insurance.[5]

The EC model of liberalization

Until the 1980s European markets in financial services had remained relatively closed despite the objective, set out in the Treaty of Rome, of creating a common market in services. The first insurance directive, on reinsurance, was adopted in 1964. The first coordination directives in banking and non-life insurance (1973) and life insurance (1979) provided the right of establishment for branches of banks and insurance companies throughout the EC. But the process stalled when it came to the more fundamental step of liberalizing the cross-border supply of services. Proposals were made, such as the Second Non-life Insurance Directive (1975), but they were not acted upon by the Council of Ministers. Nevertheless this early EC legislation provided the basis for the launch of the 1992 programme in financial services.

In the mid-1980s a combination of factors helped bring about a change in the EC. There were clear signs of a growing globalization of financial services. This made national regulation less and less viable. Divergent national regulation created distortions within the EC. The 'big bang', the liberalization of the London securities markets, created a pressure for action elsewhere. Paris and Frankfurt feared that London would further consolidate its position as a financial centre. Then there was the 1992 programme, aimed at the opening of national markets whilst maintaining essential prudential control and safeguards. Decisions taken by the European Court of Justice (ECJ) also prodded the reluctant member states into action by threatening to pre-empt political decisions in the Council and extend to the insurance sector the principle of mutual recognition that had been developed in the *Cassis de Dijon* case.[6]

Liberalization of capital movements and the SBCD

The first important decision, in July 1988, was to liberalize capital movements within the EC completely by June 1990, with temporary exceptions for Spain, Ireland, Greece and Portugal. National governments met this target and thus signalled to the private sector that they were serious about the creation of a single European financial area. The investment that followed enhanced interdependence and thus further increased pressure for policy integration in banking, insurance and securities. This momentum helped the Commission to push through its policy initiatives. The first piece of legislation was the Second Banking Coordination Directive.[7] This set a precedent for the subsequent directives on life and non-life insurance and investment services. It applied the 'competition among rules' approach by providing for mutual recognition of national regulatory and supervisory provisions and home country regulatory control, thus effectively creating a single passport for banking. The Commission later made proposals for equivalent legislation creating a single passport for investment services,[8] non-life insurance,[9] and life insurance.[10]

In line with practice in the major European countries, the SBCD provides for universal banking. The single passport will thus enable a bank licensed in one member state to provide a wide range of services through branches across the EC, including lending, deposit-taking, money transactions, trading in securities and financial advice. European banks can also undertake additional activities not covered by the SBCD, such as insurance underwriting, but on condition that they have the approval of their home member state and operate according to host country rules. This differs significantly from the established US approach, which has prevented interstate branching of banks and which separated banking and commercial or securities business (see below).

The EC approach does not constitute uncontrolled deregulation. All directives establish minimum essential supervisory rules, which are based on international rules where they exist. For example, the solvency ratio agreed by the Cooke Committee of the BIS was adopted by the European Community for the SBCD, and its equivalent proposals on capital adequacy for securities operations. There have also been directives on banking accounts, including annual accounts of foreign branches of banks, the reorganization and winding-up of credit institutions, own funds, deposit guarantee schemes, large exposures and mortgage credit.[11] By allowing banks to trade in and underwrite securities, the SBCD threatened to distort competition between the banks and the merchant banks or firms specializing in securities, because the banks would have a single passport and be able to compete in securities markets across the EC, whereas firms dealing primarily or exclusively in securities, including the large US securities houses, would not. Securities firms therefore pressed for an equivalent single passport and created a spill-over effect from reform of bank regulation into the regulation of securities. As a result the Commission was able bring forward its target date for the implementation of the investment services directive to coincide with that for the SBCD, 1 January 1991.

Because of the links between the two, there are market pressures for a merging of banking and insurance in *banque-assurance* or *Allfinanz*. There is also complementarity between the financial services offered by banks and insurance companies. For example, the life assurance policies offered today are treated as one form of saving. As in securities, the liberalization of insurance has lagged behind that of banking. Some member states, such as Germany, have operated restrictive regulation, requiring, for example, separate regulatory authorization for different classes of insurance. This has meant that separate subsidiaries have had to be created for life, motor and property insurance. Regulation of investment by insurance companies also differs. It has, for example been possible for an insurance company to invest up to 50% of its assets in securities (equity) in Britain, whereas in Germany the limit is 10%. This has had an impact on the size and structure of capital markets, which has in turn influenced corporate finance (see Chapter 4). The development of an internal market will therefore be slower in insurance than in banking but the trend is now clearly towards further liberalization along the lines of the SBCD.

Third-country provisions

The SBCD also set a precedent for third-country provisions, or how access to the EC market for non-EC companies is to be regulated. The reciprocity provisions in the Commission's initial 1988 draft were, as noted in Chapter 2, the source of intense debate with the US and other countries, largely because they left considerable scope for the Commission to exercise discretionary power. There was also a view, expounded in Brussels, Paris and Rome, that the EC approach offered more than national treatment, since non-EC financial services companies could select the member state which offered the best (most liberal) environment and supply the rest of the EC from this base. It was argued that this justified reciprocity provisions to ensure equivalent access to third-country markets for EC financial services companies. Article 7 (SBCD) was therefore added to the Commission proposals at the last moment, with the intention of providing the EC with leverage in negotiations on reciprocal market access.[12] Following the controversy sparked by the vague use of the term 'reciprocity', the EC subsequently made it clear that third-country provisions would be based on 'reciprocal national treatment'. In other words, the EC would provide national treatment to all countries that offered national treatment to EC companies in their markets.

Where EC national treatment is not reciprocated the Commission has powers to request that the authorities in the member states suspend the granting of licences to companies from such countries while negotiations are conducted to achieve reciprocal national treatment. This situation would not arise with the US, which already offers the EC national treatment. But the EC, like the US in many areas, also has powers to go beyond *de jure* to *de facto* national treatment. This is much harder to define. In the SBCD the EC defines it as treatment 'comparable to that granted by the Community to credit institutions from that third country'. In such cases the Commission's discretionary powers are limited and it must seek approval from the Council before it can even enter into negotiations with a third country. In order to remove uncertainty about how it might use this provision vis-à-vis US companies, and to reassure the industry, the Commission made it clear in April 1990 that there was no question of any attempt to exclude US companies by seeking 'mirror-image reciprocity'. At the same time the US regulatory system differs from that of the EC and, unless it is changed, will ultimately be more restrictive than the post-1992 regime.[13] This means the EC would be able to use the third-country provisions of the SBCD to challenge the restrictive elements of the US regulatory system.[14] Before discussing this challenge it is first necessary to describe the nature of the remaining barriers to market changes in the EC.

Developments in market structures
Just as the 1992 process is not only about legislative measures but about the interaction between legislation and markets, so access to the European market will be influenced by both statutory barriers and non-statutory barriers or structural impediments.

The *wholesale banking* sector in Europe has been undergoing a process of internationalization for some time. In many cases this has happened when banks providing services to companies in their home market have followed them across borders into other member states. Similar trends can be observed in commercial risk insurance as well as in business services such as consultancy, accounting and legal services. Local regulatory requirements have also encouraged the establishment of local subsidiaries. Henceforth the ability to provide cross-border services of wholesale banking or commercial insurance will reduce the need for local presence.

In *retail banking*, 'mass-risk' insurance or other services provided to individuals or small and medium-sized companies, the picture is different. It is in these sectors that the 1992 process is bringing about most change, by making an internal market in retail services credible. In financial services, for example, there have been no statutory barriers to establishment since the earlier directives of the 1970s. In this sense the EC regulatory regime prevailing at that time was similar to the current US regime. But it needed something more to convince banks and insurance companies that an internal market was on the way. That something was the decision on freedom of capital movement and the legislative programme to provide a single passport.

Once the objective of an internal market by 1992 became credible, companies moved to establish an EC-wide market presence, albeit by different means. In banking the Deutsche Bank sought to develop subsidiaries across the EC by itself. In the main it has acquired small banks but it has also bought Morgan Grenfell to strengthen its position in London. The Deutsche Bank is probably the only European bank with the financial muscle to pursue such a go-it-alone strategy. Others, such as Barclays, have followed similar strategies but on a more modest scale. Once one bank moved to establish a pan-EC presence its competitors were obliged to respond. As a result banking mergers and acquisitions (M&A) in the EC increased from 25 in 1985–6 , to about 35 in 1986–7, 78 in 1987–8 and 83 in 1988–9.[15] This M&A activity has reduced the number of potential targets and put a premium on any bank offering a branch network.

Other banks, unable to afford to develop or acquire their own branch networks, have opted for cooperation. This has taken various forms. One early concept was Europartners. This was based on cooperation between banks with established branch networks in their own home state and included the Commerzbank (Federal Republic of Germany), Crédit

Lyonnais (France), Banco Hispano Americano (Spain) and Banco di Roma (Italy). In this way the participating banks could extend retail banking services to customers in other member states through the branches of their partner banks. Other groupings, some quite extensive, have been formed on the basis of cross-shareholdings. For example, Paribas, Pargesa and Groupe Bruxelles Lambert form the core of one such group. There is also the CERUS group, run by Carlo de Benedetti, which bid for Société Générale de Belgique. The BNP (Banque Nationale de Paris) has links with the Dresdner Bank, which in turn is part-owned by Allianz, Germany's largest insurance company. There are in addition other more arm's-length cooperation agreements, such as that between the Royal Bank of Scotland and Banco Santander.

Important restructuring has also been taking place at the level of the mutual savings banks, many of which are seeking to develop into fully-fledged universal banks, first at the national and then at the EC level. For example, Crédit Agricole, which was founded to fund French agriculture, is using its extensive branch network as a basis for funding the development of other services and branches in other member states. German regional banks are also consolidating and expanding internationally. For example, West LB, the state bank of Rhineland Westphalia, has purchased the international operations of the Standard Chartered Bank. The scale of this restructuring has depended upon how fragmented the national banking sector was to start with. In Britain there has always been a relatively high degree of concentration and the banks have also already established a significant international presence. As a result there has been less restructuring in Britain than in some other member states.

There were similar developments in the EC *insurance* sector between 1986 and 1989. Mergers and acquisitions increased from 12 in 1985–6 to 28 in 1986–7 and 40 in 1987–8 before a period of consolidation (33 deals) in 1988–9.[16] Paradoxically, companies have moved to establish a local presence in other markets just as proposals are being tabled that would give them the ability to provide insurance services across borders. As noted above, there has been an explicit right of establishment since the first insurance coordination directive of 1973. What has happened in insurance, as in other sectors of European industry, is that a combination of the credibility imparted by the 1992 programme, and moves by their competitors to establish a pan-EC presence, has provoked many insurance companies to develop EC-wide strategies sooner than they would otherwise have done. The net result has been an increase in M&A activity, both national and cross-border. As in banking there are now few small targets left. This means that there is likely to be a lull until the next phase of takeovers, which will inevitably involve larger firms.

The importance of branch networks in the banking and insurance industries has also accelerated the trend towards *Allfinanz* or *banque-assurance*. As the option of acquiring a branch network by acquiring a series of medium-sized companies has diminished, insurance companies have looked to the alternative of cooperating with a regional bank and thus gaining outlets to retail customers through local branches. Again, there are some companies that will go it alone. The Deutsche Bank, for example, has set up its own insurance company. But in most cases cooperation is the route that will be chosen.

Structure and access

The 1992 programme has therefore resulted in some significant restructuring in European financial services. The need for a local presence in retail banking and the mass-risk insurance business has meant that this has generally taken the form of cooperative arrangements in banking or acquisitions in insurance. Consolidation has meant that in future it will be harder rather than easier for non-EC companies to gain effective market access. The smaller companies offering branch networks have been bought and cooperative arrangements or joint ventures set up between the European players. Established European companies will have the advantage of access to branch networks, which in turn offers lower-cost money through deposit-taking. Companies without branch networks will have to rely on more expensive sources of funding, such as the money markets. Thus while 1992 has resulted in a lowering of the regulatory barriers to the EC market, it may well have contributed to the development of structural impediments to market access. For example, it will in future be more expensive for new entrants to establish a presence in the EC market, and well-capitalized EC companies will have the financial muscle to fend off attempts to acquire market share.

Another phase of restructuring is to be expected. In banking it has been suggested that this will create some ten Europe-wide banks and a series of smaller national banks.[17] If and when this occurs there will be opportunities for non-European banks or insurance companies, but the costs of market entry will be higher than ever. The large Japanese financial services companies appear to be better placed than US banks, which have been withdrawing from the EC financial services markets. In other words, market structure will become a more important factor in market access as the regulatory barriers are removed.

The US approach to regulation

The US has a dualist system of regulating financial services, meaning that it is shared between the federal and state levels. This came about originally more by accident than design. Before the civil war the North allowed what was called 'free banking', in which a bank could be formed by showing evidence of minimum capital requirement to the chartering bank of the state. But this led to what was called 'wildcat banking', in which banks would place their main (currency-issuing) location in an out-of-the-way place and conduct most business in the cities, where they would only redeem currency at a discount. In order to curb such practices legislation was passed to tie the centre of business to the main location. This provision, which inhibited the growth of bank branching, was then carried over into the subsequent National Banking Act, passed at the time of the civil war.[18]

In the 1890 Currency Act capital requirements for banks serving small towns were reduced in order to help ensure the supply of banking services. As a result the number of banks in the US doubled from 13,000 to about 25,000 by 1910, and in so doing created an anti-branching establishment, supported by state legislation. As early as the 1920s there were efforts to liberalize these restrictive banking laws, and the Comptroller of the Currency, who regulated national banks, sought to increase the rights of national banks to branch in states that allowed it. A Supreme Court ruling in 1924 held that the state had control over branching unless the Congress legislated otherwise. In 1927 the McFadden Act anchored this division in statute and limited the rights of national banks to branch beyond the city in which they had established a subsidiary, even if the states provided for intra-state branching for state chartered banks. In other words, the national banks did not even have 'national treatment' in the states.

Bank failures were seen as one of the causes of the recession of the 1930s and there was broad support for regulatory reform. Interestingly, this prefigured the current debate in that some advocated the strengthening of banks through liberalization – including, for example, allowing more branching – and others argued for the introduction of deposit insurance. The latter prevailed and branching remained tightly regulated by the states. The 1933 Banking Act (Glass-Steagall Act) liberalized the regulation of national banks by giving them the same rights as state banks. When it came to the increasing bank involvement in securities, the act opted for caution and a simple prohibition rather than any effort to regulate such trading.

Two further pieces of legislation completed the US regulatory status quo: the McCarren-Ferguson Act of 1945 gave regulatory authority for the insurance industry to the states; and the Bank Holding Companies Act of 1956 was introduced because banks were attempting to circum-vent the ban on interstate branching by establishing bank holding compa-nies which would then acquire banks in a number of states. The Douglas amendment to the 1956 Act stipulated that acquisitions could not be made in another state unless the host state's legislation expressly permit-ted it. These acts therefore further consolidated host state control of regulation.[19] In the EC, by contrast, Article 58 (EEC) has long provided for the right of establishment throughout the Community, and the recent 1992-related directives have provided for home state regulatory control.

Little changed in the structure of US financial services until the 1980s. In 1939 there were only eighteen states that allowed intra-state branch-ing. The position in 1979 was essentially the same, but by 1981 a further nineteen states had opted for intra-state branching. As many as thirty-three states now allow bank holding companies to acquire subsidiaries in other states, twelve of these allowing nationwide banking without any kind of reciprocity conditions. Twenty-one require state-to-state recipro-city and thirteen have concluded regional agreements which allow only neighbouring states or states in the same region reciprocal access to their market. Unlike in the EC, however, there is still no interstate branching. Some liberalization has been brought about in securities by the actions of regulators, as opposed to legislators. Bank holding companies may trade in securities up to a set limit (10% of their turnover), albeit with 'fire-walls' separating securities from banking operations. Similar efforts to allow banks to engage in some insurance activities were stopped by Con-gress with the Garns-St Germain Act of 1982. Nevertheless, seventeen states authorize insurance brokerage, and five insurance underwriting.

Attempts at reform
The US system has therefore evolved over the years but it remains a complex dualist system, in which the fundamental principle of host state regulatory control remains dominant. The whole picture is further com-plicated by the fact that, at the federal level, there are three different regulatory bodies involved in the banking sector: the Office of the Comptroller of the Currency (OCC), which still regulates national char-tered banks; the Federal Reserve Board (FRB), which shares the regula-tion of state chartered banks with the states and regulates state chartered banks that are members of the Federal Reserve; and the state regulators

Table 3.1 Limits on services of commercial banks

Are banks allowed to provide these services?	Belgium	Canada	France	West Germany	Italy	Japan	Luxem-bourg	Nether-lands	Switzer-land	United Kingdom	United States
Insurance:											
Brokerage	Y	N	Y	Y	N*	N	Y	Y	N	Y	N*
Underwriting	Y	N	N*	Y*	N*	N	Y	N	N	Y*	N
Equities:											
Brokerage	Y	Y*	Y	Y	Y	N	Y	Y	Y	Y	Y
Underwriting	Y	Y*	Y	Y	Y	N	Y	Y	Y	Y*	N
Investment	Y	Y	Y	Y	Y	Y	Y	Y	Y	Y*	N
Other underwriting:											
Government debt	Y	Y	Y	Y	Y	N	Y	Y	Y	Y*	Y
Private debt	Y	Y*	Y	Y	Y	N	Y	Y	Y	Y*	N
Mutual funds:											
Brokerage	Y	Y	Y	Y	Y	N	Y	Y	Y	Y	N
Management	Y	Y*	Y	Y	Y	N	Y	Y	Y	Y	N
Real estate:											
Brokerage	Y*	N	Y	Y	N	N	Y	Y	Y	Y	N*
Investment	Y	Y	Y	Y	Y	N	Y	Y	Y	Y	N
Other brokerage:											
Government debt	Y	Y	Y	Y	Y	Y	Y	Y	Y	Y	Y
Private debt	Y	Y	Y	Y	Y	Y	Y	Y	Y	Y	Y

Key: N = No; N* = No, with exceptions; Y = Yes; Y* = Yes, but not directly by the bank.
Source: American Bankers Association, *International Banking Competitiveness*, March 1990, p. 82.

who control the state banks that are not members of the Federal Reserve. Table 3.1 shows how the US system compares with other countries and the restrictive nature of the US regulatory system in terms of what commercial banks are allowed to do.

This regulatory policy has resulted in a fragmented financial services industry in the US. For example, in banking there were nearly 14,000 commercial banks in the mid-1980s, of which the top 100 accounted for about 57% of total assets. This contrasts with Europe, where the larger EC member states have between 300 and 500 banks each, and the big banks account for most of the assets. In Britain, for example, the top five banks controlled 45% of total assets in the mid-1980s, in Germany the top six controlled 40% and in France the top three over 40%. As noted above, the level of concentration in Europe is increasing as a result of 1992.

There have been seven attempts to reform the US regulatory system since 1945, starting with the Hoover Commission in 1949. The latest was the so-called Bush Task Force, established in 1982, which reported in 1987. These efforts failed to pass the congressional hurdle. Opposition to reform has taken various forms. These have included the symbolic importance of the Glass-Steagall Act, which was passed when banking failures were seen as contributing to the 1930s recession; opposition from the securities industry, backed by the powerful Wall Street securities houses; and objections by small local and regional banks which feared the increased competition from the national banks based in the money centres of New York, Los Angeles and Chicago that would result from liberalizing interstate branching. The prospects for reform were made worse by the Savings and Loans crisis in the mid-1980s. A few years earlier the thrift business (provision of loans for home purchases) had been deregulated in such a fashion that many thrift companies were allowed to over-extend themselves. At the same time deposit guarantees were provided by the Federal Deposit Insurance Corporation (FDIC). When the real-estate market collapsed so did many thrifts – at a cost to the US taxpayer estimated in 1990 at $250–300bn dollars and rising. There is no immediate parallel between the thrifts and the banks. The latter are more closely regulated and are, for example, subject to minimum capital requirements, which the thrifts were not! The Savings and Loans scandal nevertheless created a political climate that was antagonistic towards regulatory reform.

The effects of fragmentation
The fragmentation of the US market is felt, by banks and regulators alike,

to have had adverse effects on the strength of US banks. The most often quoted indicator is that there are no longer any US banks in the top twenty-five banks measured by worldwide asset values.[20] In securities there are still eleven US companies in the top twenty-five, but the US and British dominance has been broken by Japan, led by Nomura.[21] Just as European industry argued for an end to the fragmentation of the European market, so the US money-centre banks have argued that fragmentation of the US market limits their ability to develop the scale necessary to compete on global markets. In 1983 foreign banks held 20% of the commercial and industrial loan market in the US. In 1990 this had risen to 29%.[22] One of the effects of this fragmentation has been to limit the ability of banks to spread risk. The McFadden Act requires the establishment of separately capitalized subsidiaries in each state. Consequently there has been a series of bank failures as regional banks have been caught by regional economic downturns related to the decline in agriculture or in oil. Such vulnerability should not be overplayed; after all, California is a large state and state banks in California are by no means small. Nevertheless the regulators support reform to enable interstate banking and universal banking because they believe this will, with the appropriate prudential safeguards, strengthen the banks, and thus the whole banking system, by allowing them to spread risk more easily. Finally, the existing regulatory structure is seen as contributing to the under-capitalization of US banks. Many US banks also argue that significant cost savings can be achieved by avoiding duplication of administration resulting from the requirement to have subsidiaries established in each state.

The EC's 1992 programme has come at a critical time for the debate on regulatory reform in the United States. US banks envisage growing competition from European banks once these have completed their own restructuring. There is an image of large EC banks with strong branch networks throughout Europe moving into the US market. US banks have already cut back on their operations in Europe as well as other parts of the world.[23] The 1992 provisions will also mean that the existing EC affiliates of US banks could branch throughout the EC, whereas their domestic parent could not conduct interstate banking in the US. In order to enable US banks operating in Europe to compete with European universal banks the Federal Reserve, under its so-called Regulation K, allows US banks abroad to trade in securities. Regulation K sets limits of $2m per issue, which means that US banks cannot operate as leading underwriters for major foreign rights issues. Nevertheless, the fact that US banks have operated safely under Regulation K within Europe is given as a further reason for reform of the Glass-Steagall separation within the United States.

In short, there is a view that the US is falling behind the EC. In giving evidence to congressional hearings Robert Clarke, the Comptroller of the Currency, summed up the sense of frustration among regulators and the industry as follows: 'While all of us [in the US] have been debating, analyzing, writing papers, holding hearings, manoeuvring and suing each other the EC has acted and is acting.' No doubt those who have been seeking regulatory reform in the US have used the EC's 1992 programme as a means of furthering their case, but whatever the motivation developments in the EC have had an effect on the domestic US debate.[24]

In early 1991 the US Treasury produced proposals for legislative reform.[25] These included the removal of the separation between banking and commercial/securities business, the introduction of interstate banking, a simplification of the regulatory structure and measures to limit FDIC coverage and recapitalize the Bank Insurance Fund (BIF). A form of universal banking would be introduced by allowing well-capitalized Financial Services Holding Companies (FSHCs), which would replace the old bank holding companies, to acquire or establish securities or insurance companies. The provisions of the McFadden Act preventing interstate banking would be repealed after a period of three years. The three-year delay appears to have been intended to help buy off the opposition of the smaller regional banks, giving them more time to adjust before being exposed to the competition of the national banks. The Treasury proposals leave the state legislatures to decide on whether state chartered banks would be able to engage in interstate branching. Finally the proposals picked up the Bush Commission's idea of streamlining the regulatory agencies, with the responsibilities of the OCC and Office of Thrift Supervision being assumed by a new Federal Banking Agency (FBA) within the Treasury. This would regulate national banks and the Federal Reserve Board state banks.[26] The objective is regulatory reform to end the fragmentation of the US market and thus strengthen banks and reduce the likelihood of further heavy calls on the FDIC.

Interestingly, the Treasury paper contained virtually no reference to the external implications of such reform. It was not until the draft legislation was tabled a few months later that it became clear that foreign banks would be expected to establish FSHCs if they wished to benefit from the liberalization. The European banks in the US believe that their rights should be 'grandfathered', or allowed to continue operating the bank holding companies already established, just as the rights of US banks were under the SBCD.[27] The European Commission mirrored the US response to the SBCD by welcoming the liberalizing thrust but criticized these requirements for foreign banks on the grounds that they would limit the ability of European banks to compete on the US market.[28]

The initial response in Congress was negative and many expected the reform proposals to be significantly watered down. In May 1991, however, there was a reversal of opinion in the responsible House of Representatives sub-committee, and the Treasury proposals were unexpectedly voted through more or less intact, although there was opposition to the streamlining of the regulatory bodies. The Senate Banking Committee initially showed less support, but in the summer of 1991 it seemed possible that a significant reform could be passed before the end of the year. In addition to the introduction of interstate branching, and the ability of banks to conduct securities or insurance business through FSHCs, the legislation proposed refinancing the depleted capital of the FDIC. The pressing need for this refinancing helped to give the legislative proposals some momentum.

Structure of the US market
Compared with the EC there are relatively few non-statutory or structural barriers to market access in the US. In the past European banks have been tempted to invest in the US by the scale of its retail banking and insurance markets. This investment has not always been successful, as the British Midland Bank's acquisition of Crocker in California demonstrated. But any US regulatory reform which enabled European banks to provide a universal service across the US would make the US market more attractive than ever. The fragmented structure of the US industry would also give European banks ample opportunity to acquire local branch networks, especially as US banks are relatively short of capital. It is important to qualify this with regard to the growing strength of some US regional banks. Thanks to regional interstate banking agreements, these have grown as large as, if not larger than, the current major European banks. Moreover, the merger of Manufactures Hanover and the Chemical Bank, announced in July 1991, could set a trend towards consolidation among the money-centre banks. The town or city bank is also part of the cultural picture in the US and there may be resistance to foreign acquisitions. In cases where a local bank has been taken over the desire to have a local bank has often resulted in the creation of a new local competitor. But this does not change the fact that there are few structural barriers to the US market.

US trade policy

How should the US handle the external component of any reform of its banking system? At a federal level US external policy is based on national treatment as embodied in the 1978 International Banking Act. EC banks or insurance companies operating in the US are treated in the same way as indigenous banks or insurance companies, which means they cannot, at the moment, engage in interstate banking in the US. Nor will they be able to offer the same universal banking service as they can in Europe. State regulations must be complied with but where there are reciprocal interstate banking agreements for bank holding companies, the EC bank will have the same rights as any bank from the state in which the EC bank has established a subsidiary. Access to the US market in banking and especially in insurance will therefore be determined by each host state. This is the clear systemic difference between the US and the EC, where access is determined by the most liberal state because the concept of home country control is used.

In 1990 Donald Riegle, the chairman of the Senate Banking Committee, and Jake Garns introduced the Fair Trade in Financial Services Act. This proposed measures very similar to the 'reciprocity' provisions in the EC's SBCD. Indeed it made specific reference to the SBCD as a model. As with EC policy, it too was based on reciprocal national treatment and would stretch the concept of national treatment beyond both *de jure* and, potentially, *de facto* national treatment. When Senator Riegle sponsored the Treasury proposals on banking reform in the Senate he took the opportunity of adding a reciprocity provision similar to that included in his earlier bill. This would give the Treasury and US regulators discretionary powers to deny applications from banks from countries that are judged, by the US, to discriminate against US companies.[29] The legislation brought before the Senate also reintroduced the requirement that foreign banks establish a FSHC. The motivation behind this could well yet create tension with the EC.

Apart from this piece of US legislation there should not be any immediate trade tensions in EC–US financial services. There is little prospect of the EC using its reciprocity provision in an aggressive fashion against the US. The regulatory barriers in the US do not warrant this and the trend is in any case in the direction of regulatory reform. For its part the US is likely to continue to base its treatment of foreign banks in the US on national treatment, but like the EC it will probably have powers to go beyond *de jure* national treatment in seeking access to export markets. The US has a tendency to use such provisions more aggressively. It is conventional wisdom in the US, as in the EC, that policy-makers have Japan in mind when they devise such reciprocity measures. But as noted above, structural impediments also exist in the EC, so one cannot preclude the use of reciprocity provisions against the EC in an effort to remove them. The questions for trade diplomacy then become: how does one define *de facto* national treatment, can structural impediments be considered as denying such treatment and, if so, to what extent should they or can they be covered by multilateral agreements?

Multilateral negotiations

The US was largely instrumental in getting services, including financial services, on the GATT agenda at the beginning of the 1980s. The EC was less enthusiastic about extending the scope of the GATT. It argued that there was a need to finish the work begun but not completed during the Tokyo round before extending the GATT, but it went along with the idea of including services in the work programme established after the 1982 GATT ministerial meeting.[30] Only after considerable work in the OECD and GATT was the EC persuaded that it was in its interests to negotiate a General Agreement on Trade in Services. By the time the Uruguay round was launched in 1986 the EC supported inclusion of services. Thenceforth the main problem was persuading the developing countries to participate.

The first two years of the Uruguay round involved improving statistics, analytical work on how to structure a multilateral agreement in services and trying to persuade the developing countries to participate. At the mid-term review meetings in Montreal and Geneva in December 1988 and April 1989, one of the main issues was whether a general framework agreement could be negotiated without knowing how principles such as national treatment, right of establishment and mfn status would affect specific sectors. The question was resolved by deciding to do parallel work on a framework agreement and sectoral studies, to be completed by the end of 1989. One of the other major issues was how the developing countries, which wanted the ability to develop their infant service industries, could be accommodated without repeating what was generally considered to have been the error of granting them broad exemptions on the basis of special and differential treatment, as in Section IV of the GATT.

Even at this early stage a shadow was cast over the financial services sector by the opposition of the US Treasury, and the Japanese Ministry of

Finance, to the coverage of financial services by any framework agreement. The US Treasury wished to have a separate agreement for financial services in order to ensure that the objectives of financial services regulation, such as sound banking and prudential control, were not held hostage by trade disputes in other areas, such as telecommunications. There was clearly also a desire not to lose regulatory control to national trade officials or, even worse, multilateral trade bodies such as the GATT, who were not 'qualified' to deal with financial regulation. In the EC there was less opposition from national regulators because these had already ceded a significant degree of sovereignty as a result of the EC's 1992 directives, and the EC therefore argued for comprehensive coverage for the GATS.

A draft framework agreement in December 1989 was based on national treatment, mfn status and non-discrimination. Reports were also produced on a range of sectors, including financial services. The talks then turned to how to proceed with the negotiations. Should there be positive or negative lists? In April 1990 the US and the EC agreed on the broad lines of their approach. These were that a framework agreement would be drawn up based on the draft text, to which would be added sectoral annotations dealing with the applications of the principles to each sector. Reservations for certain sectors would be possible for a time-limited period, provided they were listed in country schedules. These reservations would then be negotiated away in future rounds (the negative list approach). This would also enable the interests of developing countries to be accommodated by providing them with potentially longer transitions. There would in addition be specific commitments to liberalize (the positive list).

At about the same time as the April 1990 understanding the differences between US and EC expectations began to emerge. The US, largely at the insistence of the US private sector lobbies, wanted to see some 'red meat': i.e., immediate market-opening. The EC, on the other hand, made it plain that it would not consider negotiating on specific commitments until the shape of the agreement was clear and the question of sectoral coverage in particular had been resolved.

In addition to the Treasury there were other sectoral interests in the US that were determined to gain exemption from part of the GATS and especially from the mfn provisions. Sectors such as air transport and shipping, which had successfully gained exclusion from the US–Canada Free Trade Agreement, also wished to stay outside GATS rules. Telecommunications sought exemption from the mfn provisions because

45

they were not confident that the Uruguay round would result in concrete market-opening. There was in particular a concern that a framework agreement incorporating mfn treatment would discipline the use of US trade legislation as a means of negotiating bilateral trade liberalization. In recent years the use of such instruments has come to be seen by many in Washington as more effective than multilateral rules. The danger for these US lobbies was, therefore, that the GATS would discipline the use of Section 301 but provide no concrete liberalization of US export markets.

It is worth recalling that one of the main objectives of the EC in the Uruguay round, as set out in the Council mandate to the Commission in 1986, was to ensure that US domestic trade legislation came under GATT discipline.[31] The EC financial services lobbies, such as the European Community Services Group (ECSG), in which the British Liberalization of Trade in Services (LOTIS) committee has a leading role, pressed for a comprehensive agreement. A more sector-by-sector approach was thought to run the risk of a series of derogations undermining the whole agreement by reducing its coverage and credibility. For the EC the exclusion of financial services from mfn and national treatment requirements would have significantly undermined the value of the GATS. As OECD codes (see below) already cover elements of financial services, there was also a danger that these would be undermined by a weak GATS.

For its part the EC managed to contain its protectionist interests, although it was understood that the existing protectionist regimes in some sectors such as shipping or air transport could not be liberalized overnight. The EC, under French pressure, also sought an exemption for broadcasting, which was the cause of considerable unhappiness in the US. The EC recognized such exemptions as consistent with the negative list approach, provided they were time-limited and subject to subsequent negotiations. But in November 1990 the US negotiators argued that all US service sectors should be indefinitely exempt from the GATS mfn treatment. This may have been a tactic aimed at bringing the EC to the negotiating table on concrete commitments. But it reflected an underlying reluctance on the part of the US lobbies and Congress to see binding limitations on the use of US trade legislation, such as Section 301. In contrast the EC seemed relaxed about signing up to an agreement that would prevent it using its third-country provisions, such as Article 7 of the SBCD, in a similar fashion.[32]

At the December 1990 Brussels meeting the US delegation issued a statement to the effect that it was committed to the mfn principle but that 'this implies' that all countries make substantial commitments to market access and national treatment. The US position was that the offers made on commitments were little more than standstill agreements. The issue of sub-federal government was not resolved in Brussels. Given the importance of state regulation it was logical that the EC would wish to see this covered by GATS discipline, but the US administration was not prepared to ask Congress for legislation to constrain the states. Nor was it possible even to table a sectoral annex for financial services. A proposal from Canada, Japan, Sweden and Switzerland contained what was probably close to a consensus, including wording that defined national treatment as 'equal competitive opportunities to those available to nationals'. If this is anything to go by, the sectoral annotations seem likely to confirm the move towards *de facto* national treament, but they are unlikely to provide unambiguous definitions. How, for example, should 'equal competitive opportunities' be determined?

The GATT is not the only forum in which international negotiations on trade in financial services take place. As noted above, the 1986 agreement of the BIS on capital adequacy formed the basis of EC and US regulation aimed at setting common standards. The OECD has also developed two codes, on the Liberalization of Current Invisible Operations and the Liberalization of Capital Movements. While these have few powers of enforcement and rely ultimately on peer pressure, they have provided the fora for discussion and thus promoted cooperation (see Chapter 4).[33] The national financial service regulators would greatly prefer to use channels other than GATT to deal with the sector. As noted above, there is a strong conviction, especially among US regulators, that trade experts in the GATT will not understand the sector and that problems can be best solved by financial services regulators sitting down around a table. There may be some truth in this, but financial services, for better or worse, form an important integral part of the services sector. To take it out of the GATS would result in a collapse of the negotiations.

Conclusions

The financial services sector shows some very distinct differences between the EC and US approaches to regulatory policy. The EC's use of home country control is particularly important in this sector and has helped ensure that policy decisions have kept up with market developments in the EC. This has established a positive dynamic which has facilitated regulatory reform and a reduction in statutory barriers to

47

market access in the EC. In the US there is a dualist system of state and federal regulation, in which host state rather than home state control has predominated until now, and which has hindered reform. The US financial services industry is therefore suffering from the kind of fragmentation that the 1992 programme was designed to tackle in Europe.

Although economic interdependence in financial services has been limited mainly to the wholesale banking and reinsurance fields, it has nevertheless been sufficient to expose the US to a *de facto* competition among rules. The 1992 programme has thus increased pressure on the US regulators and policy-makers to reform regulatory policy so as to prevent US financial services companies falling further behind their international competitors. At the time of writing it is not clear how the US, and Congress in particular, will respond to this challenge. If reform comes it will reduce the regulatory barriers in the US. Access to the US market might then be significantly enhanced because of the absence of structural barriers. The interesting question will then be how US legislators respond to increased market penetration by foreign banks. In such a scenario structural impediments in the EC may in the future become the target of US reciprocity measures, especially if there is no agreed definition of what is meant by *de facto* national treatment.

The GATT negotiations on services are continuing. Although some concrete liberalization may result, this is likely to have a less significant impact on market access than the effects of changes in EC and US regulatory policy. A GATS would, however, provide multilateral discipline. The US finds such discipline harder to accept because influential lobbies expect quick results and bilateral or selective trade liberalization has come to be seen as producing them more effectively than multilateral means. Furthermore the regulatory barriers are more important in the US, whereas structural impediments are relatively more important in the EC and especially in Japan. This makes bilateral 'reciprocity' provisions more attractive than multilateral rules for the US as a means of enhancing access in these markets. Strengthening multilateral discipline tends to increase the openness of markets in which regulatory barriers predominate, such as the US, and to leave the structural impediments untouched. If agreement is reached on a sectoral annex for financial services it is likely to draw on such concepts as 'equivalent competitive opportunities', which will take trade diplomacy into the murky area beyond *de jure* national treatment.

Given the slow pace of the multilateral negotiations, are other approaches possible? The EC approach could be extended to the transatlantic or G10 setting through mutual recognition and home country control.[34] Some of the essential minimum requirements have already been drawn up, for instance on capital adequacy. But it is not clear that the kind of result that came from the BIS agreement on capital adequacy could be repeated. Regulations in each of the three major areas, i.e. the US, Japan and the EC, are at present also divergent. National regulatory authorities are unlikely to accept financial services companies from other 'spheres of regulatory influence' operating in their markets. There are also major problems in dealing with supervision. Would German regulators be responsible for the failure of a German bank that has branches throughout the US? Would US regulators such as the FDIC accept this? Within the EC there appears to be sufficient confidence in the level of cooperation between the different systems that major failures can be avoided. Would there be equivalent confidence in the G10 setting?

Given these difficulties such ambitious approaches as a multilateralization of home country control seem out of reach for the time being. But this does not mean that there will be no policy convergence. Interdependence resulting from international capital movements means there is a form of *de facto* competition among rules between the US and EC. In financial services this seems to have created something of the positive dynamic that has characterized the 1992 programme. This could well help to avoid or contain trade disputes between the US and the EC, especially if the US presses ahead with regulatory reform. The task for trade diplomacy is to promote such a positive interdependence.

4

INVESTMENT

In interdependent economies the flow of investment and policies affecting investment are of considerable importance to market access. Investment can be used to get round barriers to market access in the shape of trade policy measures, such as anti-dumping actions or quantitative restrictions on imports. It also provides a means of overcoming regulatory barriers by enabling local establishment. Finally, investment in a local presence, whether through greenfield investment or the acquisition of a local company, can offer a means of overcoming structural impediments. For example, the purchasing practices of utilities may well favour companies with local facilities that can offer prompt servicing and repairs. The acquisition of a local supplier therefore offers a means of combating such impediments. In each case it is possible to argue that such investment is 'forced', in the sense that companies are obliged to invest locally if they wish to gain effective access. The US Congress, prompted by a number of US companies, has argued that EC policies are indeed forcing companies to invest in the Community, and that market access must be enhanced by the removal of all barriers to the cross-border supply of goods and services.

In reality, however, totally unimpaired market access is unlikely to be achieved. Even within the EC local market characteristics will remain. In some cases these might be described as structural impediments. The ability to gain access by means of direct investment is therefore important, and this chapter focuses on statutory or non-statutory measures which can prevent or inhibit such investment. These can be at national or EC level in the Community. In practice there is no common EC policy towards inward direct investment, but EC policies influence such investment flows and also set the terms of national investment policies. As with financial services, there is more of a dualist structure in US investment policy, with the states and federal authorities playing an equally important role.

Investment controls

A range of statutory barriers to investment exists in the individual member states of the EC and in the US. These occur mostly in the service sector, in banking and insurance, transport or communications, and in access to natural resources.[1] Access in the former has been improved in recent years thanks to the liberalization of capital movements and financial services in the EC. Transport and communications remain more closed. Sometimes access is subject to authorization or a concession granted on a case-by-case basis; more frequently it is granted on the basis of reciprocity. Where such sectoral restrictions exist in the EC they do so at a member-state level. In the US they can occur at both state and federal levels.

Both air and maritime transport are largely closed to foreign ownership in both the EC and the US. In the US, for example, operators of civil aircraft must be US citizens. There are also strict controls on foreign ownership of US radio and broadcasting, and in telecommunications restrictions exist on foreign control of companies with a common carriage licence (in which the foreign shareholding may not exceed 20% or 25%). This became an issue in 1991 during negotiations between the US and Britain on access to the British market for US telecommunications companies, following Britain's decision to introduce further competition in its basic network services. The British argued that if US companies were to have enhanced opportunities in Britain, it was also necessary for the US to reassess such limitations on foreign ownership of common carriage. The issue has not arisen in the rest of the EC because telecommunications networks are still controlled by public monopolies. In areas such as value-added services the 1992 programme is helping to bring about liberalization, but the successors of the PTTs still dominate the market, even in Britain, and thus pose a form of structural impediment.

Table 4.1 provides a summary of the general range of impediments to inward direct investment. This shows that there are relatively few restrictions in Britain, Luxembourg and Denmark. These are followed by

Table 4.1 Position of selected OECD member countries on sectoral controls and impediments to inward direct investment

Country / Sector	1	2	3	4	5	6	7	8	9	10	11	12	13	14	15	16	17	18	19	20	21	22	23	24	25	26	27	28	29	30	31	32	33	34	35
Belgium	RI			1		M	M			M	M	M	MR									M													
Denmark				RI																			I												
France	RI	RI	R	RI	I	MR	M	M	RI	R	MRI	MR	R			MRI	MRI	RI			MRI	RI	M	M	RI		R	R	I		M				M
Germany	I				M	M	M			M	M	MRI	R													M									
Greece	RI			I	M	M	M			M	M	M	MI	I	I	I	M					M				M									
Ireland	RI	I		RI	M	M	M			M	R	R	RI	R				R																	
Italy	RI	I		RI	MR	M	M			M	R	R	R	RI	R	I	R	R		M	M	M				M									
Japan	I	I					I	MI				I	I	I	R	R	R	R	R	M	M										M	M			
Luxembourg			MI			M	M														M	M													
Netherlands	RI	I				M	M				M	R	R				M				M		I												
Portugal	R		RI			MR	M	R			M	M	MR				M				M	M	M		R						M				
Spain			MI		I	MR	M				M	R	R				M			M	I		M			R								M	I
United Kingdom	I	I	I		MR	M	M				M	R	R				M		M	I		M								M					
United States	I		I		MR	MR				R	R	R	R	R	R	R	R	R		R	R						R				M			I	

Key to impediments:

R = Sectors in which some or all activities are subject to controls or impediments regarded as restrictions in the sense of the Code of Liberalization of Capital Movements.

I = Sectors in which some or all activities are restricted by other impediments.

M = Sectors in which some or all activities are closed to investment due to public, private or mixed monopolies.

Key to sectors:

1 Banking 2 Other financial services 3 Auditing 4 Insurance 5 Press, publishing, printing 6 Broadcasting 7 Telecommunications 8 Audiovisual 9 Health and social security 10 Employment agencies 11 Land transport 12 Air transport 13 Maritime transport 14 Fishing 15 Real estate 16 Mining, metals 17 Petroleum 18 Agriculture 19 Forestry 20 Nuclear industries 21 Water power 22 Utilities (inc. water, gas, electricity) 23 Armaments 24 Security services 25 Tourism 26 Gaming 27 Legal services 28 Education 29 Merchants and craftsmen 30 Alcoholic beverages 31 Tobacco 32 Salt 33 Pharmaceuticals 34 Steel 35 Public works and services

Source: OECD, Controls and Impediments Affecting Inward Direct Investment in the OECD Member Countries, Paris, 1987.

Germany, Belgium and Ireland, with Italy and France showing the largest number of impediments. The table therefore reflects the diversity of national policies on investment within the EC, which has influenced the internal EC debate on investment issues. In general there are more impediments among the EC member states than in the US. Structural impediments or regulatory barriers in the shape of monopolies, whether private or public, are also more important in the EC. Although there are overall fewer barriers in the US, regulatory barriers appear to be relatively more important. By comparison, the EC shows both regulatory barriers and structural impediments in more or less equal measure. The table predates the 1992 directives liberalizing financial services and telecommunications and the other less far-reaching transport liberalization measures.

There are no significant barriers to investment in manufacturing in the EC. Some countries, such as France and Spain, retain general notification requirements on non-EC companies which apply to manufacturing as well as services. In Britain there are reserve powers, under the 1975 Industry Act, to prohibit foreign investment in manufacturing which is considered against the national interests, but these have never been used. The liberalization of capital flows, together with a general trend away from investment controls, means that the major impediments to investment in the EC are now in sectors in which public monopolies exist and in some services where reciprocity provisions apply. Both are the subject of GATT negotiations.

In the US there has, if anything, been an increase in the pressure to impose controls on foreign direct investment as the US has moved from being a net exporter of capital to a net recipient.[2] The highly visible acquisitions of some major US companies by Japanese companies have ensured that controls of foreign investment have become an important political issue. The Committee on Foreign Investment in the United States (CFIUS), an inter-agency committee chaired by the Treasury, was established in the mid-1970s to monitor the impact of foreign investment on US national security interests. In its first ten years the CFIUS acted against only one foreign bid, for a company manufacturing ball bearings.[3]

The Exon-Florio amendment

In congressional deliberations in 1987 proposals were made to grant powers to the US President to block foreign acquisitions if the 'essential commerce' of the US was threatened. The intent behind this Exon-Florio amendment to the Omnibus Trade and Competitiveness Act was to ensure that the US retained a national (i.e. nationally controlled) industry in certain 'strategic' sectors such as electronics. The Reagan administration and US business blocked the amendment because of its protectionist overtones, and because it clashed with existing US obligations in the OECD and ran counter to the US objective of negotiating improved multilateral disciplines on investment in the Uruguay round.

The amendment was replaced by a provision which allowed the President to prevent foreign mergers with – or acquisitions of – US firms if there is 'credible evidence' that this would jeopardize national security. The vague nature of the provision was interpreted by US observers as meaning that the President would not make significant use of the powers, although foreign investors in the US were concerned that the lack of precision could be used against them. The administration entrusted the CFIUS with the task of conducting investigations. Between 1988 and 1990 some 450 notifications were made under the provisions. Notification is not obligatory but as the 1988 Act provides for disinvestment if a merger or acquisition is subsequently found to be against US national security interests, companies have generally played safe and notified bids. In October 1990 the Exon-Florio amendment lapsed with the Defence Production Act to which it was tied, but the threat of new legislation being made retroactive has meant that companies have continued to notify. Of the 450 cases considered, the CFIUS has investigated only eleven and prohibited only one, the acquisition of an aerospace supplier by Chinese interests, on the grounds that the acquisition would have enabled the People's Republic of China to gain access to technology covered by strategic export controls. In the case of some other bids modifications were negotiated before they were allowed to proceed.

With the lapsing of Exon-Florio there has been renewed pressure for tighter, more effective investment controls. Some congressional opinion holds that the administration has failed to protect US interests adequately and a bill introduced by Representative Walgren aimed to limit the discretionary power open to the President by establishing tighter standards of investigation.[4] By mid-1991 many more bills had been introduced on the topic, including one by Congresswoman Collins that would assess foreign takeovers according to their 'impact on the industrial and technology base of the US'.[5] The fact that there are many bills being proposed reflects the political sentiment against foreign control of 'strategic technologies'. Those favouring more restrictive controls support their case by using the experience of the Gulf war, in which 'the US planes would not have been able to hit their targets without Japanese electronics'.[6] But it is by no means clear that such bills will result in legislation that is much more restrictive than the Exon-Florio amendment, and so far there has been little impact on investment flows. In Europe statutory controls on investment are becoming less important. They have, in part, been removed and where they remain in existence they are seldom, if ever, used.

Mergers and acquisitions in European restructuring

Other chapters in this volume illustrate the importance of mergers and acquisitions in the response of businesses to 1992. In order to establish a pan-EC presence quickly many companies have acquired or merged with local suppliers. In the 1970s there were few cross-border takeovers in Europe. A number of early efforts to bring about cross-border rationalization, such as that of Unidata in computing or Hoesch-Hogoverns in steel, ended in failure and tended to discredit the whole idea. Those who favoured European integration despaired at the apparent inability of European firms to bring about EC-level restructuring, and commentators argued that the competition between national champions, the fragmentation of the market and the lack of a common identity meant there was a bias against cross-border mergers in Europe and that as a result European companies were more likely to cooperate with companies in the US or Japan.[7]

There was a steady worldwide increase in M&A activity during the 1980s. Initially this showed no shift towards cross-border M&A activity. National takeovers were increasing as fast as cross-border takeovers and generally from a much higher base. In the past cross-border takeovers represented about 15% of total takeovers (i.e. national and cross-border) for the US and the EC taken as a whole. Intra-EC cross-border takeovers account for a further 15% of total takeovers, bringing the typical cross-border figure for EC member states to 30%. There is no appreciable difference between the EC and its EFTA neighbours, in which cross-border takeovers have, during the 1980s, also accounted for between 30% and 35% of all takeover activity. In comparison, cross-border takeovers in Japan have never been more than 8%.[8] There was an increase in the share of intra-EC takeovers in total takeover activity after the 1992 process won credibility: from 25% of the total in 1986–7, to 29% in 1987–8, and rising to 34% in 1988–9.[9] Private monitoring services suggest that the total value of cross-border activity was some 45.3bn ecus in 1989, of which UK companies accounted for no less than 20bn ecus of the assets acquired. The strengthening of cross-border activity continued throughout 1990, the value of cross-border takeovers in the first six months being some 30bn ecus.[10]

Competition policy and merger controls

The application of competition policy, and in particular merger control policy, can represent a potential barrier to investment where discretionary powers are used to block foreign acquisitions for other reasons. This has been an important issue in Western Europe, where merger control measures have been used as industrial policy instruments. Two broad approaches to merger control exist within the EC, one based on public interest and one on competition. Britain and France have pursued the public interest approach, which involves the extensive use of discretionary powers by national governments. In Britain the Conservative governments of the 1980s exercised self-restraint, did not use the full range of discretionary powers available and pursued policies based 'primarily on competition'. But the statutory basis of British merger policy remains unchanged and the only constraint on the pursuit of interventionist policies by another government would be those set by EC policy and statutes. Germany has pursued the competition approach since it introduced merger control legislation in 1973; unlike in Britain, its competition criteria are firmly anchored in statutes. To help ensure that decisions are based on competition rather than industrial policy criteria, investigations are also carried out by the independent Federal Cartel Office. Apart from Britain, Germany and to a lesser degree France, the other member states either have no sophisticated merger control policy at all or, as in the case of Spain and Italy, have only recently introduced one.

Until the 1980s all member states with the exception of Germany pursued policies with more or less explicit industrial policy objectives. At least merger control was seen as an instrument that could be used to help create or support national champions. Even in Germany, the last word remained with the Minister for Economics, who could overrule decisions of the Federal Cartel Office on the grounds of some overriding (political) objective. This *Ministererlass* was used only seven times between 1973 and 1989, but in that year the Daimler-MBB merger showed that industrial policy issues can still play a role.

During the 1980s there has been a general shift in European policies on concentrations (mergers) towards a competition-based approach, with restrictions on the use of merger controls as a discretionary instrument of national industrial policy. This really follows the general move away from government support for national champions. If there is no national champion policy, there is less need for instruments to block foreign takeovers. National champions may not have been targets for takeover bids but national merger controls provided the means of blocking foreign-controlled companies from gaining a presence in the domestic market and thus undermining the national champion's home base. The move to create a single market in Europe constituted a break with such policies. This shift has also been codified in EC legislation in the shape of the Merger Control Regulation, which was adopted in December 1989 and came into force in September 1990.

The first attempts to reach agreement on an EC-level merger regulation were made as long ago as 1973. They were followed by a series of revised proposals which all failed because of disagreements over policy objectives (competition or industrial policy) and over who should implement policy (national governments or the European Commission). The EC Merger Control Regulation that was finally agreed is essentially competition-based. The Netherlands, Britain and especially the Federal Republic of Germany were not willing to support a regulation that would enable the European Commission to pursue European industrial policy objectives. Consequently, earlier French-inspired drafts which provided for discretionary powers were rejected. Some flexibility remains but much less than originally envisaged by the Commission and less than currently exists under national statutes. There is arguably less flexibility in the Merger Control Regulation than in the existing Article 85(3) EEC provision of the Treaty of Rome, which the Commission was threatening to use instead, had the member states continued to block agreement. This article exempts restrictive agreements from the Article 85(1) EEC prohibition, if they 'contribute to improving the production or distribution of goods or to promoting technical or economic progress while allowing consumers a fair share of the resulting benefit.' In the Merger Control Regulation the wording on development of technical and economic progress is given less weight and hedged in by the requirement that it must be 'to the consumer's advantage and ... not form an obstacle to competition.'[11]

There is little doubt of the legislative intent here, which is that EC-level merger control should be competition-based. Of course, it remains to be seen how the EC-level controls will be applied in practice.[12] Past experience with Article 85(3), which gives the Commission greater discretionary powers, suggests that the Commission will err in favour of a narrow rather than a broad definition of the law. In the case of

57

Article 85(3), the Commission was repeatedly criticized by industrialists for being overly 'legalistic and Germanic' in its interpretation of the Treaty provisions, and not giving enough importance to the need for European industry to compete in international markets.

The main source of uncertainty is the dualistic nature of policy within the Community. EC control only applies to larger mergers when at least two of the participants have an EC-wide turnover of 250m ecus and the aggregate worldwide turnover of all the companies involved is more than 5bn ecus. Anything below this will be dealt with by national authorities. This is the result of the member states' reluctance to cede control to the Community. The member states also fought to ensure that they retained reserve powers to block any bids they consider to be contrary to the interests of 'public security, the plurality of the media and prudential control' (Article 21(3)). These powers are more or less in line with existing OECD exceptions from national treatment requirements (see below). On balance, therefore, the moves to create a common EC control of mergers should reduce the scope for the use of such control to limit foreign acquisitions. If there is a danger of industrial policy prevailing over competition policy objectives it is at the national level. But even here the trend is towards competition criteria. A codified European competition policy is better for foreign companies because it reduces the ability to use national merger controls and other instruments of competition policy to keep foreigners out.

The EC regulation contains a specific third-country provision – added, at the insistence of the French, at the very last minute. This provides for the European Commission to monitor the treatment accorded to Community undertakings in non-member countries and to report on it to the Council, in 1991 in the first instance. If the Commission finds that Community undertakings are not granted 'comparable treatment' to undertakings from non-EC countries, the Commission may seek a mandate from the Council to negotiate with 'a view to obtaining comparable treatment'. The provision therefore stops short of an outright reciprocity provision.

US anti-trust policy is based on competition criteria and it is difficult to see how it could be used to discriminate against foreign acquisitions. In recent years there has been a tendency to relax anti-trust control and thus to allow greater concentration in order to enhance the position of US companies vis-à-vis international competitors through scale economies. This found expression, for example, in the 1984 National Cooperative Research Act, which gave general encouragement to cooperation. More recently, the US administration has argued that reducing the threat of triple damages for cooperative ventures would help US competitiveness. Legislation introduced by the House Judiciary Committee in June 1991 proposed relaxing anti-trust discipline for joint ventures in order to promote US competitiveness, but on condition that there would be no more than 30% foreign participation in the venture. This is a further reflection of the political steam behind what would in Europe be called industrial policy, but the Bush administration is opposing the discrimination against foreign companies.

One other issue in competition policy is *extraterritoriality*. Under US anti-trust legislation (in the shape of the Hart-Scott-Rodino Anti-Trust Improvements Act of 1976) mergers taking place within the EC have to be notified if either of the firms concerned owns a subsidiary in the US with assets of more than $25m. This is similar to the notification requirements under EC merger policy. For example, a merger of two US multinational companies must be notified to the European Commission if they have a combined worldwide turnover of 5bn ecus and EC operations with a combined turnover of 250m ecus. Such mutual exercise of extraterritorial powers could clearly result in a conflict between judicial systems. In order to avoid such conflicts there has been consultation between national competition authorities within such fora as the OECD. A bilateral channel of communication has also been opened up following the proposal by Sir Leon Brittan, the Commissioner with responsibility for competition policy, which is described below.

In the field of competition policy there would appear to be a convergence between the EC and the US. Initially the European approach was predominantly based on public policy and a blend of competition and industrial policy objectives. The US approach was competition-based and firmly anchored in law. The codification of policy in the shape of EC statutes means the EC is moving to a more legally based approach. The US is contributing towards this convergence by making anti-trust controls a little less rigid. The discussion on reform of anti-trust policy to facilitate joint ventures in strategic sectors is also bringing the US closer to the EC approach.

Corporate control

Statutory competition policy is only part of the story. In some countries there are non-statutory barriers to takeover which are even more significant. Since effective access to certain markets, such as those in which there are structural impediments or regulatory barriers to entry, depends in part on the ability to acquire a local company, the degree to which there is an open market for corporate control can be an important factor in market access.

There are important differences between countries with regard to takeover activity and the motivation for takeovers. Within the EC there are far more takeovers in Britain than in any other country: no less than 74% of the total, according to a 1989 report commissioned by the British Department of Trade and Industry.[13] These figures are undoubtedly distorted by reporting variations, and when one considers the value of the takeovers the picture is a little more balanced, but there can be no doubt that takeovers are used much more often as a means of bringing about corporate restructuring in the UK than in other EC countries. This reflects the relatively open market for corporate control that exists in Britain in comparison with the rest of the EC. From the point of view of market access in the EC and the US it is also important to note that the United States shares this open, Anglo-Saxon market for corporate control.

There are various reasons for the difference between the Anglo-Saxon approach and what might be called a continental European/Japanese approach. First there is the size of capital markets. In Britain the capitalization of the stock market is roughly equivalent to GDP and in the US to about 60% of GDP. In France and Germany it is only about 20% of GDP and in Italy 16%. There are also a larger number of companies listed on the London Stock Exchange and US stock exchanges – 2000 and 7000 respectively, compared with only about 450 in France, 400 on the various German exchanges, and a mere 200 or so in Italy. In France and Italy few of the companies listed can in fact be bought. It has been estimated, for example, that only seven Italian listed companies have more than 50% of their shares in public hands, and of these five are controlled by families.[14] The French market is a little more open but most of the top forty companies, accounting for 63% of market capitalization, cannot be bought because of family control, cross-shareholdings or state shareholdings.

In Germany and Holland there are fewer structural barriers to takeover and shares are traded more openly, but there are barriers which make it difficult to gain effective control of companies without the approval of all stakeholders in the company. There have been virtually no hostile takeovers in Germany and on the two occasions that hostile bids have been made for major German companies, Feldmühle and Continental, there has been strong resistance from the companies concerned, with the backing of their major shareholders. Under German company law it is possible to limit voting rights of shareholders, and the Feldmühle case led to a number of companies introducing such limitations. In some cases this meant limiting voting rights to 10% regardless of the number of shares held. Such restrictions on voting rights are also possible under French company law. In the Netherlands companies have established defensive pacts, in which the participating friendly companies operate a 'White Knight' fund, buying shares in whichever of them is subject to a hostile bid. The structure of German companies also makes it difficult to gain effective control. For example, members of the *Aufsichtsrat*, or supervisory board, are appointed for 5-year terms and can be replaced only by a 75% consensus of voting shareholders. Dilution of control can also be limited by issuing non-voting shares: up to 100% of voting shares in Germany and 50% in France.

Even if the legal barriers are removed other impediments will remain. Perhaps the most important is the generally greater commitment shown by all stakeholders (often major banks) in German, Dutch and possibly French companies in the long-term growth of the company, than is shown by the institutional shareholders in Britain, such as the pension funds and insurance companies, who are more interested in maximizing their financial returns by accepting tempting takeover bids.[15] Continental management is also more able to pursue strategic acquisitions, meaning acquisitions aimed at obtaining market access, which may not show a return on investment for some time, and where it may be necessary to pay a premium in order to gain control of the company. This was certainly the case with some of the banking and insurance acquisitions in 1987–9. Anglo-Saxon managers are less likely to be able to compete in such bids because shareholders are not prepared to accept the short-term loss in dividends. Tensions have arisen within the EC between the British and the continental Europeans about the lack of a 'level playing field'. But similar tensions could well develop with the United States. The issue is now moving to the centre of the ongoing debate about market access in the Structural Impediments Initiative.

Generally speaking, the regulation of capital markets and company law in the US is similar to that in Britain and it helps to ensure that there is an open market for corporate control. Regulation is geared to protecting the interests of shareholders and tends to restrict companies or prohibit them from pursuing policies that would, for example, limit voting rights for new shareholders, so as to prevent hostile takeover bids. Recently, and especially since the last wave of acquisitions during the second half of the 1980s, there has been a growth in support for more statutory measures which provide potential target companies with some shelter against hostile bids. Some US states such as Pennsylvania and Massachusetts have introduced legislation aimed at dissuading hostile bids, both national and foreign. The experience with junk bonds has also soured the taste for leveraged takeovers. Despite all these developments the US market for corporate control remains more open than Europe's, and there are few signs of any convergence between the continental European and Anglo-Saxon approaches.

The EC has gone some way towards removing the statutory barriers to the market for corporate control in the EC. In its revised Thirteenth Company Law Directive the Commission is, for example, proposing measures that would restrict companies' ability to limit voting rights for shareholders. Unfortunately Britain, which would benefit most, is opposed because it would mean an end to the self-regulation of takeovers by the City of London Takeover Panel. Even if this directive can after all be adopted, it will have no effect on the structural differences that exist within the EC and by extension between the EC and the US.[16]

To sum up so far, national governments in the EC no longer pursue policies of supporting national champions. There has also been a shift towards more competition-based use of merger control, which reduces the scope for its use in a defensive fashion. At the same time, there is no open market for corporate control in continental Europe and some important structural impediments remain in the shape of state monopolies or cross-shareholdings between major companies. Another way of looking at this is that the continental Europeans are relaxed about foreign investment because their strategic companies are safe from foreign control. There is thus no need to seek statutory means of dealing with foreign penetration of 'sensitive' industries, and no effective pressure for EC-level controls on inward investment into the EC. In sectors such as cars France would like to limit Japanese investment, but in general terms there is little or no prospect of the EC ever reaching an agreement on a common policy towards inward investment. The divergence within the EC on investment policy is most clearly reflected in the contrast between Britain's resolutely liberal position – which even a Labour government seems unlikely to change because of the importance of foreign investment for British manufacturing – and France's continued opposition to Japanese incursions into the EC.

The US has also remained open for investment. There are fewer public monopolies, anti-trust policy is still competition-based and not accommodating towards market-sharing, and there is an open market for corporate control. At the same time, and perhaps because of this, there is pressure for statutory controls on inward investment in 'strategic' sectors. In general, however, relatively few barriers to investment exist in either the US or the EC.

Multilateral negotiations

The OECD

There are two main areas of multilateral negotiation on investment issues, the OECD and the GATT. The OECD Convention set out the objective of pursuing the liberalization of capital movements. This found expression in the 1961 Code on the Liberalization of Capital Movements, which requires member countries to grant 'any authorization required for the conclusion or execution of transactions and for transfers' of capital, including direct investment. The Code also employs the principle of national treatment to foreign direct investment and establishment.[17] Countries are allowed exemptions from this liberalization requirement on the condition that they are notified. The exemptions are then reviewed by the OECD's Committee on the Liberalization of Capital Movements and Invisible Transactions (CMIT). The OECD Codes have the legal status of OECD Decisions which are binding on member countries, but ultimately there is no effective sanction to enforce compliance other than peer pressure.

In 1976 the OECD produced a Declaration on International Investment and Multilateral Enterprises. This was in part a pre-emptive strike against the efforts of the United Nations Conference on Trade and Development (UNCTAD) to develop codes of conduct for multinational companies, but it also strengthened the OECD National Treatment instrument.[18] This requires, subject to public order and essential security, that enterprises from OECD countries

> ... accord enterprises operating in their territories and owned or
> controlled directly or indirectly by nationals of other member
> countries treatment under their laws, regulations and administrative
> practices, consistent with international law no less favourable than
> that accorded in like situations to domestic enterprises.

As for the Code, it is also possible to request exemptions for certain sectors. These are reviewed regularly and committees then make recommendations to countries – in the case of the Capital Movements Code, the CMIT. If a country decides to accept such recommendations, or otherwise liberalizes by removing reservations, it cannot reintroduce the reservation. This is the so-called ratchet effect. The Codes were generally considered to have been effective in the 1950s. During the 1960s and 1970s the ratchet effect helped to prevent regression into less liberal capital movements. But it was only in the 1980s and under the effect both of unilateral decisions by Britain and Japan, and of EC-level liberalization in the shape of the commitment to remove all controls on capital movements by 1990, that countries began to reduce the level of reservations significantly.

Revisions of the OECD Codes continued during the 1980s. In 1982 the OECD Council meeting at ministerial level requested the CMIT and the Committee on International Investment and Multinational Enterprises to review the operations of the various OECD instruments concerning direct investment in order to fill in any gaps that existed. As a result two major changes were made. In addition to notifying any existing or new measures which prevented direct investment or denied national treatment, it was decided that reciprocity requirements and the existence of other impediments such as public or private monopolies should also be notified to the OECD. Revised lists of exceptions and impediments were produced in 1984[19] and revised in 1987.[20] Table 4.1 above is based on these revised lists of exceptions. The OECD has therefore begun to move into the area of structural impediments. There has also been a programme of work on specific sectors which has underlain much of the GATT work on services.[21] These considerations resulted in revisions to the Code on Capital Movements in 1986, which extend its coverage to virtually all capital movements. The 1986 revision also requires the removal of all obstacles to the establishment from abroad of a subsidiary, branch, agency or representative office. The Code on Capital Movements therefore goes a long way towards requiring the right of establishment within the OECD area, albeit subject to the usual process of reservations. These provisions are understood to apply to the first establishment by a foreign investor. Thereafter the national treatment provisions cover the creation of new branches or subsidiaries.

In line with its desire to improve the disciplines covering international investment, the US pressed in the late 1980s for more binding OECD provisions in the field of national treatment. This objective was endorsed by ministers, who gave a mandate to the CMIT to negotiate more effective enforcement measures. These were due to be completed in 1990 in time for adoption by the OECD ministerial meeting, but no agreement could be reached. The main problem was over the inclusion of sub-national entities in binding provisions of the Codes. This was seen as important by the Europeans, and especially the British, because of the relative importance of sub-national regulatory authorities in investment policy. State regulation in the US has an important impact on investment in a range of sectors including, for example, insurance – a sector in which the EC (i.e. Britain) has a large surplus with the US. The European members of the OECD therefore wished to ensure that the sub-national regulators would not escape the tighter provisions.

The sub-federal coverage is not a new issue. Earlier revisions of the Codes included reference to the need for measures taken by a 'territorial subdivision' of a member country to be notified to the OECD in a similar fashion to national measures. But federal governments were only obliged to notify sub-national measures 'insofar as [they] had knowledge' of measures taken by the state which might restrict capital movements or inward investment. There was no obligation on the federal governments to ensure compliance with the Code.

The discussions failed in 1990 because the US seemed reluctant or unable to bring the states into the agreement. The US administration intended to implement the enhanced agreement on national treatment by means of an Executive Agreement. This would not bind Congress and could be applied to the states only if the federal government was prepared to enforce it. For the Europeans this provided no guarantee that the US Congress would not simply pass legislation which would undermine the value of the agreement.[22] Nor was the US administration prepared to commit itself to take individual states to court in order to enforce national treatment for non-US companies.

In early 1991 further unsuccessful efforts were made to reach agreement. For its part the US appeared reluctant to introduce legislation into Congress to give the Code the status of a binding treaty. This is understandable at a time when there is political pressure for legislation to introduce controls on foreign investment in certain strategic sectors which would conflict with the aims the administration is pursuing in the OECD. In order to resolve this dilemma the US administration suggested that an OECD 'Super Code' be negotiated to integrate the National Treatment instrument and the Code on the Liberalization of Capital Movements. In the negotiations the US suggested that if the Europeans accepted its best endeavours on national treatment it might put such a

Super Code to Congress. It argued (as the EC had done over agriculture) that, given the domestic political constraints because of the attitude in Congress, it was better to agree on what could be agreed today and try again later. On investment, however, it was the Europeans, and in particular the British, who considered that the US offer was insufficient and the negotiations again failed.[23]

The GATT Uruguay round
The issue of investment was reintroduced into the GATT in the work programme following the 1982 ministerial meeting. As with all the new issues, it was the US that pressed to have it put on the agenda. The US interest was to extend the GATT to provide multilateral discipline for the investment performance requirements made by host countries for foreign direct investment. During the preparations for the Punta del Este declaration developing countries came out against comprehensive inclusion of investment on the grounds that the ability to pursue national investment policies was important for their economic development. The EC's position was more cautious than that of the US. It gave general support for the inclusion of investment in the round but favoured a compromise that would limit discussions to the trade-distorting effects of investment. The motive behind this was to maintain a position which most developing and middle-income countries could accept and to limit the scope of the negotiations. In comparison the US administration, with the support of a coalition of private companies, continued to seek a more comprehensive agreement, and seemed ready to accept a GATT code signed only by a limited number of countries, rather than accepting the lowest common denominator.

Industry within the EC saw developing countries as the main source of problems with regard to TRIMs. An agreement between 'like-minded' countries in the OECD was therefore seen to be of little value, especially as the OECD work already covered most of the ground, and provided further backing for the national treatment provisions in Article III of the GATT. The US interest in a comprehensive agreement was driven by a desire to aim for an ambitious package in the round. There was also the legacy of past policy positions favouring controls of TRIMs as well as the experience of the dispute with Canada in the late 1970s and early 1980s over the Canadian Foreign Investment Review Agency, which imposed TRIMs on US investment in Canada.

The US list of TRIMs therefore extended to around fourteen measures, including some, such as local equity requirements, which the EC saw as not directly related to trade. The EC, for its part, argued for a shorter list of some six to eight TRIMs that had a direct impact on trade. The EC was supported in this position by Japan, despite the Japanese desire to strengthen disciplines on local-content provisions within the EC. Up to the mid-term review of the Uruguay round there was little discussion of details because of these differences over the scope of the agreement. The US eventually moderated its more maximalist position and the industrialized countries moved towards a consensus on the major TRIMs (local content, export requirements, local manufacturing requirements, trade-balancing requirements, production requirements and exchange restrictions). The US still wished to have a longer list that would include technology transfer requirements and equity participation in remittances. The objective of both the EC and the US was that these TRIMs should be prohibited. The EC was relaxed about prohibition because there are no TRIMs employed by the EC itself, and if national governments in the EC impose TRIMs they do so on an informal basis, without seeking written agreements. In those cases where such informal TRIMs were applied, there was a general belief that they could not be challenged in the GATT. The TRIMs not in this short list of prohibited measures would still be covered by the GATT, but discipline would be on a case-by-case basis depending on how trade-distorting the particular measure was. This approach was supported by most of the OECD countries, although Australia had problems because of its extensive use of TRIMs.

The main difficulty was therefore with the developing countries, and especially the 'hard-line' developing countries opposed to prohibition. The US brought pressure to bear on these countries during the negotiations, by including Indian investment measures in its 1989 Super 301 list of unfair measures. The Community adopted a more moderate line and sought to keep the developing countries on board.

The other issue was the nature of the final agreement on TRIMs. The US private sector coalition pushing the case for TRIMs was very keen to have a code because this would enable more to be achieved and avoid the agreement being 'watered down' by the developing countries, but the EC resisted this. In the end there was a general consensus that an agreement incorporated within the GATT would be preferable. As things stand existing GATT provisions, such as in Article III (national treatment) or Article XI (quantitative restrictions), cover many TRIMs. Indeed all but one of the short list of TRIMs (export marketing requirements) are thought to be theoretically covered by existing GATT provisions. A separate code could undermine legal certainty and introduce doubt about whether the existing GATT articles still applied. In other words, the positive inclusion of certain TRIMs in a code could mean that other TRIMs were excluded from the GATT. This would have the effect of undermining rather than strengthening the chances of developing a strong body of GATT cases on investment.

In the run-up to the December 1990 GATT meeting in Brussels a consensus emerged that there should not be a code but an agreement intepreting and clarifying existing GATT provisions. This would require more Contracting Parties to sign up, but by the end of 1990 many newly industrializing countries (NICs) and some developing countries were in fact ready to support such a strengthening of GATT discipline. The issue of prohibition was dealt with in a fashion acceptable to the developing countries by requiring the elimination of TRIMs over a transitional period. The length of this period could then be varied depending on the level of development of the country using the TRIM. Had there been an agreement on agriculture and other issues in Brussels, it seems likely that an agreement along these lines would have been reached on investment. This agreement was made possible because the expectations and objectives of the US moved towards those of the EC and other OECD countries. The US started with a maximalist position, but during the 1980s it changed from being a net exporter of capital to a net importer. Accordingly, its interest shifted from the TRIMs taken by foreign governments against US investment, to what, if anything, the US should do about controlling inward foreign direct investment. Hence the debate on Exon-Florio and other measures discussed above.

Whatever the outcome of the GATT and OECD talks it seems certain that the issues will not all be resolved this time around. There will continue to be negotiations on investment. Indeed many of the other GATT issues such as trade in services are essentially about establishment and national treatment and thus investment.

Conclusions

Cross-border mergers and acquisitions in Europe, which started in the early 1980s and accelerated as a result of the 1992 programme, have undermined the exclusive position of the national champions on their home markets. National governments have done little, if anything, to stop this process, and have accepted or been forced to accept more liberal investment policies. At a sub-national level, regional authorities or local governments have competed in attracting inward direct investment. At the same time some leading companies could be seen as *de facto* national or European champions in so far as they have pursued strategic acquisition policies while retaining defences against takeover. More generally, the continued need for a local presence for effective market access in the EC after 1992 means that the absence of an open market for corporate control could be more of an impediment to access than any EC investment policy. The shift towards EC control of mergers should also mean greater rather than less predictability in the use of merger control. Differences between the member states of the EC and competition between the different sub-national regions even within each member state means that a common policy on foreign direct investment into the EC is unlikely to materialize. The more important question with regard to investment in the EC is whether active policies by the Community will remove structural impediments in the shape of monopolies or closed markets for corporate control.

A further issue, of particular importance for the US, is that of 'forced investment'. There is growing support for the view that the EC is forcing companies to invest within its market and thus seeking to attract more than its fair share of investment. The early 1990s are likely to be characterized by a shortage of investment. The transformation of the East German, Central European and Soviet economies, combined with the reconstruction in the Gulf states and the requirements of the developing world, as well the need for the US to continue to fund its budget deficit, all means that demand for investment is likely to outstrip supply. The EC represents a large and growing market and major international companies wish to be present in it. US critics of the EC argue that it is using policies such as rules of origin or the threat of trade protection in order to 'force' companies to invest in local production and distribution. This chapter suggests that there is no evidence of any common EC policy designed to attract investment. The size of the EC market certainly attracts investment, but it is the existence of local market characteristics, which will persist after 1992, and the concomitant need to have a local presence in order to gain effective access, that are more important factors in attracting investment than any coherent strategy on the part of the EC.

There is a spectrum of US views on investment, ranging from a concern that the EC is attracting too much investment to a concern that too much investment is going into the US, especially into 'strategic industries'. The US market is more homogeneous, so that the requirement to establish a local presence is less important. In the US there are fewer structural barriers to investment, an open market for corporate control and relatively few sectors with public monopolies. *De facto* monopolies still exist, of course, such as in the regional utilities and telephone companies, but the relative absence of structural impediments helps to explain the growing pressure for more statutory controls on foreign direct investment.

The current rhetoric on investment controls should not, however, be overplayed. The US is, and is likely to remain, open to foreign direct investment. Within the EC the trend is towards a more rather than a less liberal approach in all the policy areas affecting investment discussed above. There appears to be somewhat less direct policy interdependence than in financial services, but there does seem to be some policy convergence, as in the EC's move towards more codified, competition-based policies and the desire of the US to inject more flexibility into its policies in the form of, for example, more encouragement for joint ventures in high-tech sectors. In general terms, therefore, there are no major barriers to investment in either the EC or the US. Tensions brought about by issues such as Exon-Florio have, to date, had more political than economic impact, and the scale of transatlantic direct investment continues to grow.

5
PUBLIC PURCHASING

Public purchasing in industrialized countries accounts for between 8% and 12% of GDP. This can be broken down into three general categories: purchasing by state and local government, which accounts for about 70% of all 'government purchasing' in the EC and the US; purchasing by central government departments; and purchasing by bodies which benefit from special or exclusive rights granted by public authorities. The main components of this latter category are the utilities, energy, telecommunications, water and transport. There are significant differences between the EC and US approaches to purchasing, beginning with the definition of what is 'public'. By 1992 the EC will have a comprehensive system, with directives setting out purchasing procedures and providing remedies (bid protest) in cases of non-compliance. In international negotiations the US has tended to see 'government purchasing' as purchasing by central government and publicly owned entities only, and to exclude purchasing by private regulated utilities.

EC–US tensions in this field date from at least the early 1970s and stem from systemic differences. The US has targeted the use of preferential national purchasing in the telecommunications and heavy electrical equipment industries. This pressure resulted in the GATT Tokyo round negotiations on government purchasing and the efforts to improve the GATT provisions on subsidies. Although a Government Purchasing Agreement (GPA) was concluded in 1979, and included a requirement for national treatment and non-discrimination, it had a limited effect on market-opening because barriers to market access in purchasing are primarily non-statutory and seldom set out in legislation.[1] The agreement also only covered central government purchasing entities.

The EC's approach to the Tokyo round talks was shaped by its own internal efforts to change the established structures of supply and purchasing practices, which favoured indigenous companies. During the 1970s neither the EC nor the GATT was able to include the utilities in their liberalization measures. As a result no balanced liberalization, especially one including telecommunications and power, was possible in either. Nor could they develop effective enforcement measures. Efforts continued in the GATT to extend and improve the GPA, but it was not until the mid-1980s that major changes began as a result of the combined effects of the EC's 1992 programme and market-led pressure for change. As in the 1970s, multilateral negotiations have coincided with developments within the EC.

Non-statutory barriers in Europe

Barriers to market access in Europe are almost exclusively non-statutory in nature. The Treaty of Rome, in Articles 30 (EEC) et seq., prohibits quantitative restrictions on trade and other equivalent measures within the EC. 'Buy national' procurement policies constitute measures of equivalent effect and there are no statutory 'buy national' requirements in the EC like the federal and state-level 'buy America' laws in the US. There have, however, clearly been policies of supporting national suppliers when placing public contracts.

Purchasing practice, by both publicly and privately owned entities, promoted national suppliers while maintaining a diversity of supply. This created national oligopolies, especially in the supply structure for the utilities, and thus fragmented the European market and led to surplus capacity. Close links between national suppliers and their major clients resulted in the development of differing national design standards. These factors combined to make each national market essentially closed to foreign competition.

During the 1970s the EC introduced directives aimed at liberalizing procurement. These set out common procedures for the award of contracts and enhanced transparency by requiring tenders for contracts for central and local government above specified thresholds to be advertised in the *Official Journal of the European Communities*. It was therefore theoretically possible for suppliers, backed by these treaty provisions, to bid for public contracts in other countries and in the event of discriminatory practices to take the offending member state to the European Court of Justice. In practice, however, little changed. Purchasers continued to prefer using a limited number of suppliers with whom they had close contact and who produced to national design standards. The 1970s directives left considerable flexibility for purchasers and also loopholes through which they could avoid complying with the EC-prescribed procedures.[2] The remedy for non-compliance was recourse to the ECJ via Article 169 (EEC) for general non-compliance with the treaty. This was a long-winded procedure and too distant from the aggrieved supplier to have much effect. Finally, the EC provisions excluded the utilities because the mixed ownership structures made it impossible to reach political agreement on the regime to be introduced for these sectors. Even where EC directives applied, suppliers simply did not see market-opening as credible and were therefore not prepared to waste time bidding for contracts they knew would go to domestic suppliers.

Industrial restructuring

The position began to change in the mid-1980s, largely as a result of industrial restructuring, and was subsequently complemented by the seven directives of the EC's 1992 programme. The industry-led change came about because the national champions created by the segmentation of the European market recognized that they could not compete internationally. The costs of research and development and surplus capacity meant that cross-border rationalization was becoming unavoidable. But old habits die hard and the national champions were reluctant to link up with one another in this way. In some cases restructuring was forced on them when non-EC companies entered the EC markets and disrupted the established oligopolistic structures.

In general the restructuring is expected to create two or three major Europe-wide suppliers. In telecommunications these are likely to be Alcatel, formed by the acquisition by the Compagnie Générale d'Electricité (CGE) of ITT's European business; Siemens, which has effective control of GEC Plessey Telecommunications (GPT); and Ericsson. Smaller companies such as Telenorma (Bosch) have also moved to establish a Europe-wide presence.

In the heavy electrical equipment industry ASEA of Sweden precipitated the change by acquiring the Swiss–German Brown-Boveri group to form ABB. This was followed by the GEC-Alsthom (Franco-British) merger. ABB subsequently extended its presence in Western Europe through links with Ansaldo and Franco Tosi of Italy, and acquired East German and Polish companies in order to have a presence in the potentially lucrative markets of Central and Eastern Europe, where major investment in infrastructure is needed. These groups, along with Siemens, will form the core of the heavy electrical equipment industry in Europe. Each will be pan-European rather than national, but the continued existence of non-statutory barriers to a greater or lesser degree means that they must, at least in the short to medium term, achieve this by acquiring a local presence in each major market.

The key change, however, is that the companies supplying European public procurement contracts are no longer 'national champions' in the sense that they operate from secure national markets from which all other suppliers are excluded. This is not to say that some governments do not continue to support their home-based companies. Restructuring has not stopped at the EC's borders. European companies have also entered into cooperation agreements with Japanese and US companies, such as the General Electric (GE) links with GEC-Alsthom and ABB links with Westinghouse. ABB is clearly developing a global strategy, including acquisitions in the US through Combustion Engineering, and Siemens is establishing a presence in heavy power equipment and telecommunications in the United States.

The EC's approach to liberalization

The other major change that has taken place in Europe, the EC's 1992 programme, has been both comprehensive and intrusive. It involves the regulation of contract award procedures in all forms of 'public' purchasing, including purchasing by private utilities providing public services under licence. The EC's programme consists of: revising the two previous directives dealing with the purchase of contracts for supplies (products) and public works (construction) by central and local government;[3] harmonizing national remedies (bid protest procedures) for central and local government purchasing;[4] extending the coverage of EC directives to the previously excluded utilities;[5] the introduction of remedies in the utilities field;[6] and two directives on the liberalization of procurement of services – one for central and local government, and one for the utilities.[7] It is necessary to understand the basic approach used in the programme because this has influenced the Community's position in multilateral negotiations.[8] The EC's approach is based on three principles:

comprehensive coverage; flexibility in regulation; and effective compliance by the provision of access to remedies for aggrieved suppliers.

Comprehensive coverage
This has meant extending coverage beyond central government to include all forms of local (sub-federal) government, the utilities, whether publicly or privately owned, and services. Local government was included in the directives of the 1970s when the utilities were excluded because of opposition from privately owned German utilities, which refused to be subjected to procedures designed for 'government' purchasing. Countries with large publicly owned utilities, such as France, Italy and Britain, were not prepared to open their markets to German suppliers without having equivalent access to the German market.

When the Commission drafted the utilities directive, at the end of 1987, it also had to consider privatized British utilities such as British Telecom and British Gas. Significantly, the British government backed comprehensive coverage because it recognized that without it there could be no agreement and no chance of liberalizing purchasing in these key sectors. The German federal government, however, continued to argue against coverage of its private utilities on the grounds that these faced (substitution) competition. For example, the power sector competed with gas, and rail transport competed with roads and inland waterways. In the 1987–8 debate this German opposition was overcome, thanks to the existence of qualified majority voting, and coverage was based not on ownership alone but on the provision of 'special and exclusive rights'. In other words, it is assumed that exclusive rights granted by a regulating authority to a utility could be used as a means of influencing procurement decisions and that all such utilities, whether public or private, should therefore be covered by the treaty.

The second major extension of coverage involves the purchasing of services by central and local government and utilities. Here the EC has adopted a two-tier approach. Services that are important or relatively easy to liberalize are contained in the list of priority services for which procurement must follow common contract award procedures set out in the proposed directive. Such priority services include the purchase by central and local government of transport, telecommunications, architectural services and financial services for which fees are paid.[9] The second tier would be made up of residual services, including legal services, education, health and social services, and would be subject to less rigorous provisions. The Commission's clear intention is to get these latter services

75

Box 5.1 North Sea oil and gas

The offshore operation in the North Sea posed particular problems. The oil and gas companies operating in the North Sea lobbied hard for exclusion because they were private companies and operating in a competitive environment. The Commission firmly resisted exclusion because it viewed the operation of the British Offshore Supplies Office (OSO) during the 1970s as a classic example of the use of leverage, gained from the ability to grant exclusive rights to explore and develop the North Sea oil and gas reserves, as a means of influencing purchasing decisions.

After long negotiations a compromise was found. In Article 3 of the directive member states were given the option, when implementing the directive in national laws, to free upstream oil and gas entities from its detailed provisions, provided the member states undertook to *ensure* non-discrimination in purchasing. The obligation is expected to require intrusive monitoring by national governments to ensure compliance and avoid actions in the European Court of Justice. As a result even Britain, which asked for the provision in the first place, has not yet decided whether to use this option.

This approach has also been proposed as a means of getting around similar political difficulties between the EC and US in the GATT negotiations. But whereas the EC provision imposes a *requirement* on the national authority granting special or exclusive rights to ensure non-discrimination, the US idea for the GATT imposes no such requirement but seeks only 'self-denial' on the part of regulatory agencies.

on the agenda for future action. The services directive was being intensively discussed in the autumn of 1991 and a further similar directive was being prepared to cover purchasing of services by the utilities.

Flexibility in regulation

This was found to be necessary in order to accommodate current commercial practices. Ever since the 1970s all EC directives have provided for alternative forms of tendering: open (public notification and tendering); restricted (on the basis of a list of approved suppliers); and negotiated (with selected candidates from an approved list). There are detailed provisions covering the operation of each of these, including how candidates for approved lists are chosen. The Commission generally sought tighter provisions but was opposed by suppliers, and particularly purchasers, who argued that intrusive bureaucratic controls would inflate compliance costs and be counter-productive. The industry argued that for capital investment efficient, commercial purchasing practices require close links with suppliers. In the end a balance was reached in which the directives aim at ensuring competition among candidates to become preferred suppliers, but the political weight of purchasers backed by national governments has ensured that the alternative means of tendering remain.

Effective compliance

This third principle was to be ensured not by heavy bureaucratic control but by providing aggrieved suppliers with effective remedies. To this end the Commission sought powers to suspend contract award procedures in cases where the non-discrimination provisions of the directives had been violated, but was opposed by industry (both suppliers and purchasers), which feared costly delays, and by the member states, which feared the general accretion of powers by the Commission. Powers to suspend contract award procedures were therefore left with the national implementing authorities, which were allowed discretion to waive them 'where their negative consequences could exceed their benefits'. The other 'classic' remedy of seeking damages after the award of contract remained. The Commission was successful in retaining limited powers under a so-called 'corrective mechanism'. This enables it to bring infringements to the notice of the member states, but if these fail to respond the only recourse for the Commission is to Article 169 (EEC). The effectiveness of the compliance directive will depend heavily on the willingness of suppliers to initiate cases against purchasers when they feel there has been discrimination. This raises the question of whether companies will be prepared to bite the hand that they hope will feed them with future orders. Taking legal action is somewhat alien to the European purchasing 'culture', though not to the American, and it is not certain that suppliers will be prepared to act.

Compliance in the utilities field poses special problems because of the existence of privately owned companies. For example, purchasing by utilities – whether publicly or privately owned – in Germany and Spain is governed by the private law of contract, and intervention by public authorities, even if it is to enforce compliance, has been considered as 'unconstitutional'. The Germans therefore argued that remedies against utilities can only take the form of post-contract award damages or possibly informal conciliation. In order to get round this problem the Commission proposed various alternatives including the use of a procurement audit or attestation procedure to augment damages. The option of attestation was included in the Council directive, as indeed were provisions on dissuasive payments in cases of infringements during contract award procedures.[10] The directive does not contain any powers for the Commission to suspend contract award procedures. As for central and local government purchasing, remedies in the utilities field will depend upon aggrieved suppliers challenging contract award decisions in the courts. Given these limitations in the compliance directives and flexibility in the procedural requirements, the directives are unlikely, by themselves, to bring about an opening of the EC procurement markets. They may, however, add credibility to the objective of market-opening and thus, together with the industry-led change, bring about a liberalization.

Third-country provisions
The EC regime covers considerably more 'public purchasing' than the existing GATT provisions. Contracts for the supply of goods, works and services to central, state and local government as well as utilities will ultimately be covered. The only major areas to be excluded are defence procurement (although even here the Commission is considering what it can do), certain services and airlines.[11] The exclusion of airlines may be seen as significant, given the importance of aircraft in the US trade surplus with the EC, but the scale of Boeing sales in the EC led to an assumption that competition existed. The EC programme will also introduce remedies at all levels of purchasing. The greater coverage of the EC regime meant that some member states, led by France and Italy, but with strong support from the European Parliament, argued for reciprocity with third countries.

The utilities directive
Third-country provisions are included in the utilities directive and in the two services directives. In the utilities directive a 50% origin test and a 3% price preference were proposed. After opposition from the liberal member states the proposals for origin became optional. That is, a purchasing entity *may* disregard the directives when a bid is made by a producer of goods which are less than 50% of EC origin.[12] After some debate the price preference stayed at 3%. Although the origin rule nominally applies to all producers, whether EC or not, it is clearly against the spirit of national treatment. Such an origin test is not included in the revised supplies directive because the GATT GPA, which covers more or less the same sectors as the EC supplies directive, explicitly prohibits the use of origin rules. As utilities lie outside existing GATT provisions the EC provision, like similar US provisions, is not in breach of GATT.

These third-country provisions were the cause of controversy within the EC and prevented agreement on a common position on the directive in December 1989. The Germans and British opposed them, whereas the French and Italians favoured them. The Germans were concerned about liberal trade, but more importantly about the fact that some German suppliers to other EC markets could fall foul of the test as they source a high percentage of components from outside the EC, especially in electronics. The British were unhappy about third-country clauses, but decided to support the directive as a means of beginning the process of liberalization in the EC. The EC also recognized the link with the GATT round by providing for the third-country provisions to be reviewed in 1991 in the light of the GATT negotiations, and followed the US approach by requiring annual reports on market access granted to EC companies by third countries.

The services procurement directive
Here the Commission's proposals use the SBCD approach of reciprocal national treatment (see Chapter 3). Accordingly the Commission may initiate negotiations with third countries if they (a) do not grant Community undertakings effective access comparable to that granted by the Community to undertakings from that country; (b) do not grant national treatment or the same competitive opportunities as are available to national companies; or (c) grant undertakings from third countries more favourable treatment than Community undertakings (Article 40 COM(90)372). The last case is interesting in the light of bilateral agreements reached between the US and Japan, for example, on public construction projects. If the directive is adopted the Commission will have powers to retaliate against US suppliers of services to EC public bodies should US bilateral agreements discriminate against EC suppliers. The Commission's draft of October 1990 leaves the decision largely in its own hands, although any member state would be able to ask for a qualified majority vote in the Council of Ministers on a Commission decision implementing a third-country provision. The third-country provisions for the utilities directive caused a storm of protest and indignation in the US because they were seen as discriminating against US suppliers and keeping the EC market closed. The later proposals on services have not received the same attention.

A predominance of statutory barriers in the US
The US market is a large and – in some of the key sectors, such as telecommunications and power plant – unified market. In Europe each national PTT had developed distinct national design standards for the telecommunications network. In the US AT&T ensured a uniform stand-

ard across the continent. In the power industry too the major US producers, General Electric and Westinghouse, produce standard technology products for the whole continental market. The common language also reduces the need for local affiliates and local market presence. In this sense the structural barriers in the US are lower than in the EC.

Rationalization of the US supply industry has not been held up by a fragmentation of the market. For example, in 1987 there were twelve boiler-makers in the EC but only six in the US, ten manufacturers of turbine generators in the EC but only two in the US, eleven manufacturers of telecommunications public switching equipment in the EC against four in the US, and sixteen locomotive manufacturers against two in the US.[13]

In certain sectors the US market has generally been more open than the EC. For example, in heavy electrical equipment the US was importing some 20% of installed generating capacity during the 1980s, compared with about 3% in the larger EC member states – although this was largely accounted for by Northern Telecom, the Canadian origin company. The smaller EC member states had no national champions and limited domestic capacity and thus imported between 25% and 40% of their requirements. The US industry has suffered from a significant decline in domestic orders for heavy power plant. During the 1980s orders all but dried up. US companies also faced stiff competition on export markets in the developing world as European companies sought to ease the problems of slowing domestic orders for new plant. As Table 5.1 shows, the US has progressively fallen behind Germany, Japan, Switzerland and even Britain in export sales of power plant.

In telecommunications the deregulation of the US industry and the disinvestment of AT&T brought about a significant opening in the terminal equipment market but the US market for switching equipment remained largely in the hands of North American suppliers.

Unlike the EC, the US retains a significant number of statutory barriers to market access, as if to compensate for the relative absence of non-statutory barriers. Many of these are based on national security. For example, the Department of Defence (DoD) is prohibited from purchasing foreign goods in a range of items despite bilateral Memoranda of Understanding with the NATO partners and the GATT GPA. Special metals, machine tools and even stainless steel fall into this category. In an effort to support the domestic machine-tool industry the US Congress passed legislation in 1986 requiring any government-owned operation under DoD control to purchase US machine tools. Since 1986 the DoD no longer buys foreign bearings; its total demand for bearings at that time

Table 5.1   World export producers of power plant (measured by installed capacity in MW)

	1955–64	1965–74	1975–84	1985+
FRG	10,298	25,254	40,622	39,992
Japan	2,434	24,991	57,895	29,386
Switzerland	7,369	19,172	20,812	25,406
UK	12,582	20,924	22,452	21,129
USA	10,033	20,002	20,793	18,615

Source: SPRU Power Plant Data Base.

was some $770 million.

The 1933 'Buy America' Act (as revised in the 1988 Omnibus Trade and Competitive Act) provides a 6% price preference for US products for most federal purchasing. In other words, 6% is added to the quoted price of a non-US supplier before comparison of bids. Under the 1979 Trade Agreements Act which implemented the Tokyo round GPA, however, the President, on the recommendation of the US Trade Representative (USTR), may waive these Buy America provisions for signatories of the agreement. A range of higher Buy America preferences also exist: for the purchase of steel for the construction of federal highways (25%); for federal-supported mass transport purchasing of steel (since 1982) and rolling stock (since 1987) (25%); and high-voltage power equipment for federally controlled power utilities (since 1986) (30%). There is also a domestic content requirement of 55% on mass transit systems, to be increased to 60% in 1991. The European Commission counts a total of 'at least 40' Buy America provisions at federal level.[14] Last but not least, state and local government purchasing, which accounts for 70% of total 'government' purchasing, is also laced with Buy America provisions, especially in the construction and mass transit systems. Some 37 states have Buy America legislation.

Contract award provisions

There is no uniform procedure for the award of contracts in the US, nor any effort by the federal government to create a harmonized system. In some cases there are no procedures at all. At the *federal* level the US has a set of contract award procedures. These are more exacting than the relatively flexible approach of EC directives and thus potentially less

81

open to discretionary/discriminatory interpretation. Contractors and federal purchasing agencies must follow procedures set out in the Federal Acquisition Regulation (FAR) (48 Code of Federal Regulations (CFR)).

When it comes to *state and local government* levels, however, no uniform contract award procedure exists. Some states have adopted provisions very similar to the FAR, but they have done so in an effort to counter not just preference for local suppliers but also criminal corruption. Most states have their own procedures; some have no formal procedures whatsoever. The further one moves down the scale of local government the less formal these become.

Finally, in the case of the *private utilities* there remains in the US, as in the EC before the utilities directive, no common contract award procedure. Purchasing is seen as part of the private sector and it is generally argued that the regulating authorities, which set charge rates etc., regulate the utilities in such a fashion that they cannot afford to buy from anyone but the most competitive suppliers. This means that US utilities can, for example, set their own standards and specifications and develop close links with suppliers. For large capital projects it is normal to use a negotiated tender procedure, whereby the potential supplier is chosen by the purchasing utility from a list of qualified suppliers. Open tendering is used for lower-priced, large-volume items. Indeed one of the problems with opening 'public' purchasing markets is that, as the purchasing professionals argue, the establishment of close links with suppliers is the most cost-effective means of purchasing capital equipment.

In the EC there are requirements to use European or international standards where they exist and national standards where they do not, because the use of technical specifications constitutes a technical barrier to trade. The absence of 'agreed standards', whether national or international, in the US makes this even more problematical (see Chapter 6 for a discussion of technical standards).

Potential suppliers to the US must therefore contend with very different conditions depending on the purchasing entity. Despite various initiatives to develop codes for state and local purchasing, such as the proposals by the American Bar Association in the early 1980s, the diversity remains. At local government level there is also great variation; in some cases the mayor decides who gets the contract. Small local contracts may not be very important for international trade but the variety of contract award procedures constitutes in itself a barrier to market access.

As in Europe there are remedies for aggrieved suppliers. Again, these vary according to the level of government. At the federal level they are detailed and a range of options is provided. For example, the Comptroller General of the United States can carry out investigations into cases of discrimination. The General Accounting Office (GAO) has long undertaken investigations but this was given a statutory base in the Competition in Contracting Act (CICA) of 1984, subsequently amended in 1987 (4 CFR Part 21). The CICA also requires each executive (federal) agency to employ a person to encourage competition in purchasing. In the field of computer and telecommunications purchasing there is also a General Services Administration Board of Contract Appeals (GSBCA). This differs from the GAO in that it is judicial in nature and consists of a three-judge panel which sits to resolve disputes and protests. There is appeal from the GSBCA to the US circuit court. Finally, any disappointed supplier can ask the courts for a temporary restraining order or injunction to stop a contact award procedure when the purchasing agency concerned has not followed procedures, provided the supplier can prove that it would have won the contract had the violation not occurred and that the placing of the contract would cause irreparable harm.

As described above in the debate on remedies in the EC, the national governments and industry were strongly opposed to such contract suspension provisions, and fought to ensure that the discretionary powers awarded to the national implementing bodies would mean they were not used. Again, when one turns to the state and local level, the remedies offered vary and there is, of course, no remedy in the case of private utilities. The position in the US therefore seems even more confused than it was in the EC before the introduction of the coordinating directives.

US policy towards third countries
The US has a range of policy instruments with which it can pursue market access issues affecting public purchasing. These generally fall under Section 301 of the 1974 Trade Act, as amended, which can be used to threaten retaliation if public procurement markets are not opened up. Section 301 authorizes presidential action to enforce international trade agreements and to respond to discriminatory action by third countries whose *practices* are 'unreasonable' and deny 'fair and equitable market opportunities'. Under the revised 1988 version of Section 301 an investigation may be petitioned by either the USTR (self-initiation) or an interested party. The USTR decides whether an investigation takes place, except in cases of intellectual property. For two years after the 1988 Act there were also so-called Super 301 actions, in which the USTR had less

discretion. If unreasonable practices are found retaliation may follow, in the form of denial of access to the US market for products from the country concerned. Since Section 301 refers to trade practices, the fact that there are no statutory 'buy national' policies in the EC does not mean that the US could not use such provisions. Indeed the heavy electrical equipment industry has been trying since the 1970s to persuade the USTR to initiate an investigation into the public procurement of power equipment on the basis of 'buy local procurement practices and policies'.[15]

Following the failure to include heavy electrical equipment, telecommunications and transport equipment in the 1979 GPA, the 1979 Trade Agreements Act implementing the Tokyo round required the President to study the implications of not including these sectors and to report to Congress on 'actions deemed appropriate to establish reciprocity with major industrialized countries in the areas of government procurement'. In its report in 1981 the USTR listed eight possible remedies, including increasing Buy America provisions for entities not covered under the code. The USTR's recommendations in November 1981 were: to negotiate for an extension of coverage of the GPA; to provide credit support for US exporters; and to prepare a GATT Subsidies Code complaint on the grounds that procurement practices were equivalent to domestic subsidies. The USTR also suggested that, if no agreement on extension of coverage of the GPA was reached by the beginning of 1985 (i.e. after the review of the GPA), it might be appropriate to extend coverage of Buy America legislation. There was no agreement in the GATT on extension, and in 1986, as we have seen, a 30% price preference on purchases of heavy electrical equipment was introduced. The GPA was improved in 1988 but not extended.

The Buy America Act was modified in the 1988 Trade and Competitiveness Act. The price preferences remained but there was some fine tuning aimed at strengthening the hand of US negotiators. The general view of Congress was that the GATT GPA was not working. Rather than tighten the Buy American provisions, however, it elected to pursue a policy of 'reciprocity'.[16] The Act establishes a comprehensive scheme whereby the Executive Branch must report to, and consult with, Congress on foreign compliance with the GATT GPA. As with the Section 301 provisions in general, there are mechanisms to enable unfair practices in other countries to be identified, through an annual report to Congress. It also provides powers for the President to impose sanctions on a signatory of the GPA if he finds that the country concerned is not in good standing with the GPA as a result of 'a significant and persistent pattern or practice of discrimination' that results in 'identifiable' harm to the US. In such a case the USTR must seek redress through GATT dispute settlement. If this does not reach a conclusion within one year the President must revoke the Buy America waiver for the code signatory concerned. A 50% origin test is used to determine conformity with the Buy America Act, and there are special provisions for determining the origin of contractors in the construction sector.

Telecommunications

The US has made specific efforts to open the EC telecommunications markets. In 1986 it initiated Market Access Fact Finding (MAFF) talks with the EC. These were conducted with the member states as well as the European Commission, and focused on the exclusion from the procurement process of foreign manufacturers lacking a physical presence in West Germany, as well as a range of regulatory policy issues affecting access to the network. At the time Congress was toying with the idea of using the Federal Communications Commission (FCC) to deny type approval authorization for telecommunications equipment from countries which denied US suppliers equivalent access. This threatened to result in US retaliation against Siemens, and was an important factor in the decision taken in 1986–7 to liberalize German telecommunications regulatory policies, which in turn opened the way for EC common policies.[17] In 1986–7 attempts were made to bring the FCC into trade policy by giving it powers to block registration of foreign products from countries which do not provide reciprocal access. These failed but registration or approval of products for connection to the US networks may be denied if certain information is not supplied to the FCC. The FCC can therefore collate information on purchasing. Similar provisions enabled the British Offshore Supplies Office to exert covert pressure on suppliers by the implicit threat of withholding licences.

The 1988 Trade Act also contains a provision on sectoral reciprocity in telecommunications based on 'mutually advantageous market opportunities'. Efforts to use these as the basis for 'mirror-image' reciprocity, which would have required the removal of, for example, public monopolies, were blocked by liberals in Congress. As with Section 301 and the Buy America provisions, the telecommunications provisions require reports to be made to Congress on market access.[18] In its 1989 report the USTR identified the EC as a 'priority country' for the purposes of the telecommunications section of the Act, and discussions began with the EC. In early 1990 the President decided to extend the discussions for a further year, rather than recommend retaliation, as progress was being made in liberalizing the EC market, and because of the ongoing GATT negotiations on the extension of the GPA and negotiations on the inclusion of telecommunications in the GATS. If no progress is made, and the President so decides, he can take retaliatory action in telecommunications goods and services, i.e. impose sectoral reciprocity. This may include prohibitions on federal purchasing of products, increased domestic price preferences or a suspension of the Buy America waiver provision for GPA signatories.

It is clear that the US domestic trade legislation provides more than enough powers to implement a policy of reciprocal market access based on 'mutually advantageous market opportunities'. Once again, this definition of reciprocity takes US policy beyond *de jure* national treatment and into the murky area of *de facto* national treatment. At issue are not transparent statutory measures but purchasing practices. This is a case in which policy vis-à-vis the EC is already driven by a US desire to remove barriers which must qualify as 'structural impediments'. In the past industrial lobbies working through Congress have sought to tie the administration down and ensure that if no progress is reached in GATT negotiations alternative measures will be taken. They can be expected to argue for the same in any legislation implementing the Uruguay round.

The GATT negotiations

The GPA formed one of the three main non-tariff barrier codes negotiated during the Tokyo round (the others being technical barriers to trade, and subsidies and countervailing duties). The EC's position during the Tokyo round was influenced by its inability to reach agreement on coverage of utilities. Since the US did not wish to cover state or local government purchasing, the coverage was limited to supplies of goods (but not public works contracts) to national/federal government agencies. Table 5.2 compares coverage of the GATT code with that of the EC.

The 1979 GPA is based on national treatment and non-discrimination. It contains fairly detailed provisions concerning the need to comply with recognized contract award procedures. These posed no problems for the US federal agencies or for the EC. There are also provisions on transparency which were likewise similar to the established EC and US federal provisions.

The 1991 negotiations on an improvement and extension of coverage of the GPA are not a formal part of the Uruguay round but are linked. If

Table 5.2 Coverage of EC and GATT provisions

	Central govt.	Local govt.	Utilities	Compliance/ bid protest
Supplies	EC GATT	EC	EC	EC GATT
Works (i.e. construction)	EC GATT	EC	EC	EC
Services	ECp	ECp	ECp	—

Note: p denotes proposal under discussion.

the round were to fail the prospects for making progress in the GPA would be reduced. On the other hand, as the final results of the round form a package, 'concessions' on other elements of the round may help to remove blockages in the GPA. The issues in the negotiations were already well established before negotiations began. The US sought to extend coverage to include telecommunications and heavy electrical equipment, and to strengthen enforcement measures. The EC argued for coverage of state and local government and the removal of Buy America legislation. As in the internal EC debate, the Community argued for comprehensive coverage to include all utilities regardless of ownership. The EC also supported more effective compliance measures.

By the time of the GATT mid-term review meeting the modalities of the negotiation were agreed. Three groups of purchasing entities were subject to negotiations:

Group A, central government entities, which were already largely covered by the existing GPA, although there was still scope for extending coverage;

Group B, regional and local government, where the onus was on the US and other federal countries to agree to a coverage of sub-federal level government; and

Group C, other entities whose procurement policies are substantially controlled by, dependent on, or influenced by central, regional or local government.

Group C mainly involves the utilities which, whether publicly or privately owned, are generally subject to regulatory control because they are natural monopolies. A key question in this group was what constituted 'substantial control' and the means by which government might exercise control. These were considered to include ownership (including mixed ownership), financial assistance (i.e. capital investment), special status (monopoly rights, licences etc.), rate regulation, government budget review, etc. In terms of sector coverage the objective was to extend coverage to public works contracts and service contracts as well as goods.

The EC was first to submit a full proposal, in August 1990. This effectively sought an extension of the EC regime to the GATT. Coverage was to be comprehensive and to include goods, works and services for central and regional government, and goods and works for the utilities. All utilities which benefit from special or exclusive rights were to be covered, so that the EC's offer included all entities covered by the EC directives. It also requested coverage of all the major US energy utilities, the regional holding companies of the Bell Operating Companies and their regulated affiliates as well as AT&T and GTE, all the major urban transit companies, all the major airports and an unspecified list of water utilities.

The US proposal, submitted in September 1990, offered minor extensions and adjustments to federal-level coverage. It proposed that any extension to sub-national levels should concentrate on the first level below the federal government, but that this should be reviewed after eighteen months. In reality the US position was that it would seek to persuade the states to amend legislation in order to comply with the GPA and would return to negotiate on the basis of what it could offer. Compliance by the states would remove the state-level Buy America provisions.

The US interest in gaining access to EC telecommunications and power equipment markets is focused on the coverage of group C entities. Here the US has proposed two sub-groups: a sub-group I, covering entities under government *control*, and a sub-group II, for entities under government *influence*. The first would include entities which were *both* publicly owned or operating under public law *and* benefiting from exclusive or special rights granted by governments. The second sub-group would cover entities which met one but not both of these conditions. In other words, a publicly owned utility which was nevertheless subject to competition would come under group II, as would a privately owned utility benefiting from exclusive or special rights. Group CI entities would be covered by the GPA. For group CII entities governments and regulatory agencies would exercise self-denial, i.e. not impose restrictions or obligations on entities to buy locally. But governments would not be *required* to increase their influence over procuring entities for the purpose of carrying out the obligations of the agreement. The EC interpretation of this approach is that it is a way of ensuring coverage of most EC utilities, which would fall into group I, but avoiding any obligation with regard to US utilities, which come under group II. The Article 3 alternative used in the EC's utilities directive was seen as the model for self-denial. But the Commission argued that unlike the US proposal, Article 3 *requires* the national authorities to take action to ensure enforcement, i.e. to maintain supervisory powers.

If no agreement can be found to include utilities the EC and the US may revert to their respective third-country provisions. For the EC this means that, subject to review in 1991, the third-country provisions in Article 29 of the utilities directive will become operational in January 1993 and could be followed by the services directive covering construction contracts. For the US it will mean that the pressure to implement the Section 301, Buy America and telecommunications sectoral reciprocity provisions of the 1988 Act will increase.

Even if an agreement can be reached the EC–US systemic differences make it very difficult to see how this could be a comprehensive agreement based on clear (GATT) rules or principles. It is far more likely to be a piecemeal approach aimed at balancing requests and offers, as happened in the Tokyo round. The initial package seems likely to exclude sub-federal purchasing because it will take the US administration some time to determine how many of the states will comply. The EC is looking for 80 per cent of the states to sign up.

This leaves utilities in group C. Here the scope for negotiations is further narrowed by the unwillingness of the US to consider anything but its target sectors of telecommunications and power plant. It is not happy about offering anything on oil and gas or urban transport, where major investment programmes are under way. Any agreement therefore looks likely to be limited to some improvements in federal purchasing coverage, partial coverage of utilities and a strengthening of bid protest, although there are difficulties in agreeing on effective compliance measures in all areas. Such a modest package is unlikely to make multilateral market-opening credible in the short to medium term. Market-led factors may be at work at the multilateral level as well as at the EC level, but policy lags too far behind.

The absence of a clear set of multilateral 'rules' means the emphasis will be on 'reciprocity' rather than on comprehensive compliance with GATT rules. Enhancements to the compliance/bid protest provisions may help. Both the EC and the US agree on the need for GATT-level bid protest provisions and there is no major problem for purchasing in group A. The problems are again with sub-national entities and utilities. Bid protest can apply only to purchasing covered by the GPA. For sub-national purchasing a common bid protest provision based on GATT could inject more transparency into the US system, if the states were prepared to accept it, which seems unlikely. As regards utilities, the US would like to extend bid protest, but on the condition that self-denial applies to the group II entities, i.e. all but three or four US utilities. The EC argues that as self-denial places no obligation on the national government or regulatory body, such as the FCC, to ensure non-discrimination, bid protest in such cases would be ineffective. Another problem is the US position that bid protest should include powers to suspend contract award procedures, which is unacceptable to member states of the EC. There must therefore be some doubt that an effective bid protest procedure for the GATT will emerge.

Conclusions

This chapter has shown again how structural impediments, in the shape of purchasing practices, have a greater relative importance than statutory measures in the EC. The reverse is the case in the US, where Buy America provisions are the focus of the policy debate. As in investment there is also pressure in the US to achieve reciprocity through the use of statutory measures, such as through a strengthening of Buy America provisions for high-voltage power equipment or in the telecommunications section of the 1988 Trade Act.

Reciprocity provisions are also available in the EC. It has, however, adopted a comprehensive approach to opening 'public' procurement. This was necessary for political reasons in order to obtain a balance of benefit between member states with different structures of public ownership and control. It was also based on the view that only a comprehensive approach would make market-opening credible. Such credibility was necessary if suppliers were to challenge barriers to market access. This comprehensive approach has, however, required that EC legislation remains relatively flexible so as not to impose undue compliance costs on purchasing entities. In contrast the US national approach is for tightly drafted legislative requirements for a narrow field of purchasing, namely federal government purchasing. Outside this area there is a large diversity of legislation, and no formal procedures for utilities exist.

These factors have influenced the respective approaches to multilateral efforts at liberalizing procurement. The EC has sought to extend its regime to the multilateral level. The US has a much narrower focus. As a result the GATT has currently reached about the same position the EC was at during its negotiations in the 1970s. Negotiating positions are based on narrow national interests and there is no willingness or ability to accept a large package that would enable a balanced outcome. Until more ambitious proposals can be made it is difficult to see how the GATT can become really credible in this field.

In the absence of a credible multilateral regime there will be pressure for bilateral actions. The US, in particular, may revert to the Section 301, Buy America or telecommunications provisions in the 1988 Trade Act. If the precedent of the 1979 Trade Agreements Act is anything to go by, legislation implementing the Uruguay round (assuming the round can be concluded) could well require the use of such bilateral instruments. The EC will also implement its third-country provisions in the utilities directive. Such an escalation of trade disputes is not inevitable: during the 1980s the MAFF helped to defuse pressure for action in the US Congress. The objective must be to continue talking until another round of negotiations can be held to extend coverage to purchasing at sub-federal level. This could help to create the kind of package that would be needed to produce a balanced, credible GPA.

6
TECHNICAL STANDARDS AND CERTIFICATION

Technical standards and certification are areas of major importance for market access but have been neglected by policy-makers and industry except at the level of specialists. As a result decision-makers have generally been ill-prepared for dealing with the challenges presented by international standard-making. There are three main issues: the impact of divergent voluntary standards; the impact of technical regulations enacted at various levels of government; and the mutual recognition of testing and certification carried out to gauge whether a particular product complies with a standard or technical regulation.[1] As in the other case-studies we have examined, markets, in the shape of the development of new products and services, have been outstripping the ability of policy-makers to draw up standards.

The EC and the US have responded differently to this challenge. Within the EC there has been a concerted effort to reform policy-making in order to ensure that this policy-lag does not result in the continued use of national standards and divergent technical regulations which create barriers to market access. In the US the role of public policy has been limited to technical regulations, such as in the fields of safety or the environment, and the responsibility for ensuring that standards and certification are adequate has effectively been left to industry and private bodies. As a result there is a tendency for structural impediments to be more important in the US and regulatory barriers more important in the

EC. Technical barriers in the US assume more of a structural nature in that they do not result from national regulation but from the dominance of standard-making by the leading companies. The top companies in any given sector can, by determining the product standard, influence market access, especially when interconnectability or compatibility with a national design standard is important.

The 'privatization' of national standard-making policy in the US means that it faces a major challenge when it comes to interfacing with international standard-making, which is dominated by the European standards institutions.[2] The EC member states form the core of a European standard-making process which already includes EFTA and is seen as a model by the Central and East European countries. The reform of EC policy in recent years has also made European standard-making more dynamic and efficient. Not satisfied with this, the EC Commission has proposed further changes, in the shape of its October 1990 Green Paper (detailed below), in an attempt to ensure that policy keeps pace with economic integration in Europe. This effort at a regional level has put the EC in a very strong position to influence the multilateral discussions. In comparison US standard-making energies have been channelled through the private sector and individual companies. As a result the US presence in the international standards bodies – the International Organization for Standardization (ISO) for general standards, and the International Electrotechnical Commission (IEC) – is relatively weak. To the US these appear to be European-dominated bodies, offering no real alternative to national, private-sector-led standard-making.

As in other sectors there is an issue of market access at the sub-federal level in the US since neither state nor local government bodies are subject to the GATT provisions covering technical barriers to trade negotiated during the Tokyo round. Nor are private entities, such as the utilities or Regional Bell Operating Companies (RBOCs), subject to any national, let alone international, discipline on standards. The traditional arm's-length approach to standard-making in the US means that industry-led standards, i.e. those determined by one or a few leading companies, tend to prevail.

In the EC there has by contrast been a desire to ensure that there are genuinely agreed standards. This stems from a number of factors. First, there is a stronger tradition of standard-making in European countries. Second, the existence of a range of different national standards is costly for European industry and perpetuates market fragmentation. Third, there was a desire to ensure that there were also agreed standards at an international level and that industry standards set by US or Japanese firms should not put European companies at a disadvantage.

The EC approach

The desire to remove technical barriers to trade resulting from national legal requirements has led to significant efforts to harmonize standards in the so-called regulated sector in the EC. When harmonization failed to keep pace with market developments the EC adopted its 'new approach' (see below) to help speed things up. EC legislation applies to all levels of government. But agreement on the 'new approach' directives was in itself not enough. To ensure genuinely open markets the EC has also felt it necessary to create genuine European standards. For example, as noted in the previous chapter, a genuine opening of public procurement markets requires common European or international standards to replace national design standards in such sectors as telecommunications or energy. The EC has therefore also actively promoted standard-making.

The EC has sought to ensure that the common market was not fragmented by national technical barriers to trade that limited market access. Such barriers generally took the form of national regulation covering health and safety or environmental standards requiring the use of national standards. To this end major efforts were made to harmonize provisions fully. Between 1968 and 1985 some 270 directives establishing harmonized technical regulations were adopted. Despite these efforts the EC failed to keep up with market developments because directives took years to negotiate. In the absence of agreed EC provisions national technical regulations were still being introduced and most of the efforts in standard-making went into developing national rather than European or international standards. As a result national standard-making outstripped European standard-making. By the mid-1980s there were only 1,250 European standards (against 9,400 international standards in the ISO), whereas national standards ran into tens of thousands. There are, for example, some 20,000 DIN (Deutsches Institut für Normung), 13,000 BSI (British Standards Institute) and 10,000 AFNOR (Association Française de Normalisation) standards.

The 'new approach'

During the 1980s the EC developed a 'new approach' based on mutual recognition of national standards and certification. Under the new approach EC legislation confines itself to laying down the essential minimum requirements to which products must comply in order to ensure the protection of public health or safety, of the environment or of the consumer. European standards are developed in respect of each directive in order to provide manufacturers with a set of technical specifications recognized in the directive as giving a presumption of conformity to the essential requirements. The European standards concerned, the so-called 'harmonized standards', remain voluntary: manufacturers are still able to put on the Community market products which either meet other standards or meet no standards at all, subject to fulfilling the procedures for assessment of conformity laid down by the directive.[3] There was also an effort to channel the standard-making effort away from national work towards work on European standards by establishing an EC-level 'filter' (the Information Directive) through which all national standards must pass.

This new approach did not come about as a result of political leadership but rather because of bottom-up pressure from industry seeking more effective standards. Within industry the pressure came from the technical/scientific staff and seldom from board-level management which, outside Germany, seldom recognized the importance of standards. Nor did it come out of the blue but evolved from work under the old approach. The origins of the new approach go back at least to the Low Voltage Directive (LVD) of 1973, which was in turn modelled on the 1968 German *Gerätesicherheitsgesetz* (Law on the Safety of Equipment). This introduced the concept of delegating competence to standard-making bodies rather than trying to harmonize standards in directives negotiated in the Council of Ministers. The approach was possible with the LVD because a significant number of agreed standards already existed as a result of the work of the IEC.* Thus the EC was able to adopt the international standards, but even then they were not comprehensive enough. As a result European industry pressed for a strengthening of CENELEC in order to speed up the writing of standards in this and other areas.

The new approach was given a major impetus by the decision of the European Court of Justice in the *Cassis de Dijon* case. Ruling in a case against German technical regulations which excluded French exports of blackcurrant syrup initiated on the basis of Articles 30 et seq. of the Treaty of Rome (measures having equivalent effect to quantitative restrictions), the ECJ established the principle of mutual recognition of

*The IEC is the international equivalent of the European Committee for the Coordination of Electronic Standards (CENELEC). In the field of general, non-electrical standards the international body is the International Organization for Standardization (ISO), and the European-level body the Committee of European Standards (CEN).

national standards provided 'essential minimum requirements' are satisfied. Not for the first time in the evolution of the internal market, the ECJ therefore played an important part in forcing the political debate in the Council of Ministers. But the principles on which the *Cassis de Dijon* case were based were already being developed in the member states themselves. The British had introduced ideas similar to the *Gerätesicherheitsgesetz* in a 1982 White Paper on International Standards and Competitiveness and were also in 1985 to employ a similar approach in their revision of building regulations.

The model for the new approach directives evolved during the drafting of a directive on simple pressure vessels and consists of the following elements: a definition of the scope of the directive, i.e. the classes or types of products covered; the essential minimum requirements set out in a general clause; methods of satisfying these requirements, such as by compliance with a voluntary technical standard; safeguard provisions to be used when, for example, a product on the market is subsequently found to be unsafe; and certification and testing procedures which are to be mutually recognized.[4] These directives at the EC level replace national regulations. By the end of 1989 eight new approach directives had been adopted, covering a wide range of sectors; for example, the Machinery Safety Directive encompassed sectors in which there were previously hundreds of national safety regulations. The new approach could also be said to incorporate enhanced decision-making procedures for EC directives. The Single European Act, ratified in 1987, introduced qualified majority voting for the relevant directives. This meant that one or two member states could no longer hold up decisions on directives.

The experience with the first directives suggests that the new approach has, if anything, led to too much haste in decision-making.[5] In a number of cases the Council of Ministers, under pressure from the Presidency and Commission to adopt directives in order to keep up the momentum of the 1992 programme, has effectively ducked important policy issues and thus pushed them down the line to be sorted out by the standard-making institutions. A related problem is that the new approach directives prohibit restrictions on goods which meet minimum requirements, but there are, at present, not enough technical standards to facilitate compliance testing. Courts will therefore have few guidelines for determining, in cases of dispute, whether products meet minimum essential requirements. Industry sees this as a lack of legal certainty; some member states, notably Germany, have seen it as irresponsible deregulation.[6] The effect of this uncertainty has been to concentrate the minds of industry and standards authorities alike on ways of making the standard-making process more efficient.

European standard-making

The European standard-making bodies date from the 1950s but the current institutions from 1961, when CEN and the European Electrical Commission (CENELCOM) were established. In 1973 CENELCOM became CENELEC. In 1987 the European Conference of Post and Tele-communications Authorities (CEPT), which consists of the national PTTs and used to determine European telecommunications standards, established the European Telecommunications Standards Institute (ETSI). This was able to provide direct access to the standard-making process for industry, including non-European firms, and users. CEN and CENELEC are composed of representatives from the national standard-making institutions from the EC and EFTA countries only.

Standards are drawn up by *technical committees*, usually on the basis of a draft from one or more of the national standards institutes. Generally speaking the institute that produces the first draft will also be given the secretariat for the technical committee of that standard. The national drafts are developed in the national technical committees, which are made up of the respective trade associations and company representatives. Any member of the standards institution, including US or other foreign-owned companies, can participate in the national technical committees. In practice most of the work is carried out by a few key people from companies that are prepared to commit resources to the task. Despite the institutional structures the expertise of individuals can play a major role in the development of a standard. There will generally be one or two experts who develop the initial draft of a standard in national standards institutes. These often carry over their expertise into the European standard-making process and have in some cases had an important role in the thinking behind EC directives.

As the DIN has tended to generate more drafts it has also acquired more of the *secretariats*. In the mid-1980s it was responsible for about 35% of the 212 active technical committees, compared with about 18% each for the BSI, AFNOR and UNI (Unione della Norma Italiana). This apparent German dominance has been the source of political tensions but should not be exaggerated. Control of a CEN/CENELEC secretariat means the ability to influence the pace of standard-making rather than the nature of the standard, although this can sometimes be important. Within

97

the EC there is no doubt that German industry, and more importantly German consumers, place more emphasis on standards than industry or consumers in other member states, although the 1992 programme has helped to raise awareness throughout the EC.

CEN and CENELEC use international standards where they exist, rather than duplicating. Any national institute drafting standards which clash with international ones is unlikely to succeed in having them adopted as European standards. Within CEN and CENELEC standards are adopted by qualified majority voting. There is also a two-tier system: if no agreement is reached with all countries participating there is a recount of only the votes from the standards institutes of the EC member states. With both the EC and the EFTA countries voting it is quite possible for a standard to be adopted despite opposition from three or maybe four EC member states. This makes blocking tactics very much less effective and has created a desire to seek consensus and compromise that has greatly enhanced the speed of decision-making.

European standards bodies are independent, voluntary bodies and not subject to EC control. In order to improve coordination between EC directives and standard-making, procedures have been developed which enable the European Commission to give a mandate to the standard-making bodies identifying the areas in which standards are needed. It is also possible for EFTA to provide mandates. Some 30 mandates for standardization, covering approximately 800 standards, have been given to CEN/CENELEC since 1986. This total will soon reach 1,000.

One example of the application of the mandate is in the area of public utilities. As discussed in Chapter 5, effective market-opening in the sectors of energy, transport, telecommunications and water depends, in part, on the replacement of national design standards by common technical standards. Therefore in order to achieve the 1992 market-opening objectives in public purchasing the European Commission mandated CEN/CENELEC to work on the required standards. At present about half the work of CEN/CENELEC is related to EC mandates. The rest are initiated, as in the past, by the members of the national standards institutions operating through their respective organizations. The 1984 General Guidelines for Cooperation between the EC and CEN/CENELEC set out the conditions for cooperation, and the 1985 Framework Contract detailed the financial support that the Commission agreed to provide for work in mandated areas. The Commission is not involved in decisions on the standards themselves.

Another vital element of the EC's approach to standard-making has been the EC 'filter' for national standards regulation. In 1980 the Commission proposed the establishment of an enhanced notification procedure. This was finally adopted in 1983 as the so-called Information Directive (189/83). This requires national standards regulation to be notified to the other national standards institutes, which then have three months to comment on the proposals. The task of notification is in fact carried out by CEN and CENELEC. The idea is that if a regulated national standard is proposed which threatens to undermine an established European, or international, standard or create a technical barrier to trade, the other member states have an opportunity of commenting on – and making recommendations for changes to – the draft. If such a clash appears likely or if the European Commission believes that the introduction of a national technical regulation would be inappropriate, it can decide to produce an EC directive covering the area. Between 1983 and 1989, 766 draft technical regulations were notified to the EC, 268 from Germany, 150 from France, and 70 each from Britain and Denmark. About one-third of the drafts submitted were modified to avoid trade barriers or clashes with existing provisions. The Information Directive has therefore played a major role in improving transparency and containing the growth of competing national technical regulations.

The Commission's Green Paper

In October 1990 the European Commission published its Green Paper on the development of European standardization. The objective was to make standard-making more efficient. The Commission recognized the progress made in CEN/CENELEC but argued that more had to be done if a lack of agreed standards was not to jeopardize the achievement of a genuine internal market by 1993. The Green Paper is only a consultative document and it has not received unqualified support from the standard-making bodies in the EC. It proposed speeding up the drafting of standards by using 'project teams' or even consultants to produce drafts of standards for the technical committees to consider. It also recommends majority voting in the technical committees on proposed draft standards: at present they work until they reach a consensus on the draft. In one of its more controversial proposals the Green Paper argues that, as all interested parties have an opportunity of participating in standard-making, and given the availability of information on standards work in progress, there should be a reduction in the six-month period of public enquiry once a draft standard has been adopted. It also recommends that European standards should become immediately applicable and not require 'transposition' into national standards, which usually takes another six months.

The Green Paper proposes the creation of a European Standardization System governed by a European Standards Council, consisting of representatives of industry, consumers, users, trade unions, the EC Commission and the EFTA Secretariat. This would be responsible for the overall policy of European standardization. There would be a European Standardization Board, initially made up of the various standards bodies (CEN, CENELEC and ETSI), which would act as an executive. Under the Board would be the standardization bodies, which would be largely autonomous but subject to recognition by the European Standards Council and to overall policy direction from the Council. This system would allow greater flexibility by providing scope for new standard-making bodies in specific sectors. Finally, national bodies would 'carry out particular tasks on behalf of the European standardization bodies'. Although there is broad support for the objective of strengthening European standard-making, national standards institutes fear it will be at their own expense.

The Green Paper covers relations with third countries and international standardization bodies. It argues for a direct representation of European standards bodies in the ISO and IEC rather than the current indirect representation through national bodies. The Commission envisages building on the recently concluded arrangements on consultation procedures between the European and international bodies. It advocates a division of labour with the international bodies such as the ISO over the development of standards, but warns that international standard-making will not succeed unless 'all parties concerned [and especially the US and Japan] act with the same commitment to international standardization as Europe has done in the past' and 'implement international standards at the national level'.[7] Finally, the Green Paper stresses the importance of integrating East European countries into the European standard-making procedures.

Testing and certification

Agreement on a common standard as a means of establishing a common technical specification is only part of the picture. Equally important is the mutual recognition of procedures used to assess conformity of a product to a standard. There are various means of doing this and in its so-called

'Global Approach to Certification and Testing', in 1989, the EC provided for a choice between different modules, ranging from a manufacturer's declaration to quality assurance systems or independent testing and certification.[8] The modules that may be used to satisfy an EC directive will be laid down in that directive and be the same for both EC companies and non-EC suppliers. Thus if a manufacturer's declaration is sufficient this will hold for all suppliers. The Commission argues that it also applies national treatment, as required in the 1979 GATT Code on Technical Barriers to Trade, where products must be certified by a 'notified body'. Where there is no regulatory requirement, i.e. in the case of voluntary standards, mutual recognition applies. That is, any product can circulate freely throughout the EC, provided it has been recognized by an EC national body, whether through testing within the member state itself or through the mutual recognition of test results carried out in, say, a US test laboratory.

The problems in EC–US trade arise in the regulated sector, i.e. where standards are laid down in EC regulations, in contrast to voluntary standards. In the US both industry and administration are concerned that mutual recognition in this sector, previously granted by the national regulatory authorities, is now passing to the EC, and the Community has said it will decide on mutual recognition of foreign tests for the whole of the EC. The Council Resolution of 21 December 1989 sets the Community the objective of promoting international trade in regulated products through mutual recognition agreements, while ensuring the competence of the foreign test centre and reciprocal treatment for EC test centres. Finally, the Commission is keen to see the establishment of a European organizational framework for testing and certification equivalent to the European standards organization which would then decide on mutual recognition of test results. At present there is no coordinating body for testing and certification at an EC level.

The US approach
The US approach can be best described as 'pluralistic'. As noted above there is little or no attempt to keep national standard-making up to speed with market developments. Standard-making has effectively been privatized: it takes place through a large number of privately owned standards institutes financed by industry. There are some 250 major standards developers, of which only 17% operate through (i.e. notify their standards to) the American National Standards Institute (ANSI). Certification

is also carried out through a network of private laboratories. Any company wishing to participate in these standard-making processes is able to do so, provided it contributes to the costs. In practice there is a tendency for the leading companies in the field to set industry standards. Thus there is little to protect smaller companies from standards set by companies such as AT&T or IBM. Such industry standards can have a major impact on the access to a market.

This 'privatization' of US standard-making is in direct contrast to the European approach, and the divergence helps to explain US criticism of the EC standard-making process. The US at one stage asked for a 'seat at the table' of European standard-making.[9] This seems to have been the result of a misplaced assumption that European standard-making was carried out the same way as in the US. The EC response to the challenge of keeping up with rapidly developing technology has been to speed up decision-making and to shift from the national to the European level in order to prevent national standards creating technical barriers to trade. In the EC 'industry standards' are seen, like national standards, as potential barriers to market access, because they provide opportunities for companies which create *de facto* standards through their products to achieve or maintain market dominance by manipulating product standards to their own advantage.

This European view is illustrated in its most extreme form by the long-running competition case between the European Commission and IBM. The Commission argued that by refusing to release details of its system architecture, IBM was abusing its position of market dominance in the EC. European manufacturers of data-processing equipment saw IBM as using a *de facto* industry standard to its own benefit by refusing to provide information on the specifications of the standard concerned. Although this may stretch the definition of a standard further than most US observers would accept, it provides an interesting angle on the debate about technical barriers because the EC acted against IBM through competition policy.[10] In other words, technical standards can help create structural impediments to market access, which can be effectively countered only by the combined use of competition policy and standard-making.

This private 'industry standard' approach at a national level has meant that the US has to date tended to neglect international standards. This has created difficulties in dealing with the interface between US and international standards. Indeed it is somewhat ironic that the US administration and the more nationally based companies only began to recognize the importance of standards as a result of the 'fortress Europe' debate. When the European countries pursued national standards these were generally far more restrictive than the current EC approach to standard-making. The change to greater emphasis on European standards policy served as a catalyst for a much wider interest in this area of policy in the US than was previously the case. The introduction of mutual recognition for voluntary standards in the EC means that a US product needs to be certified as meeting EC minimum essential requirements only once, rather than, as before, having to satisfy the national requirements in each of the twelve member states. Despite this general liberalization there is some concern in the US that European technical regulations may require higher standards than is currently the case in some member states.

Unlike the EC, the US makes very little use of international standards. European critics of the US system argue that by 1989 the US had fully implemented only seventeen of the 9,000 or so ISO standards through US national standards. This assertion is rather misleading, since many of the national standards vary only slightly from ISO standards, but even minor deviations are not accepted in the EC because of the scope these provide for setting specifications that preclude foreign products.

There are a number of reasons for this neglect of international standards in the US. First, standards are accorded a generally low priority. There appears to be a vicious circle in which national standards are seen to be far behind technological developments, which results in their neglect and a further widening of the gap between the level of standards development and current technological developments.

Second, there is a genuine reluctance to accept the standards of the ISO because of its in-built voting bias. The 'Europeans' have 18 votes (EC plus EFTA), as opposed to the single vote for the US. This advantage, combined with the more extensive standards work done by the Europeans, enables them to dominate international standard-making. Put more cynically, it has been difficult to pursuade US companies to become more active in a system in which they are likely to have less say than the Europeans.[11] The EC proposals in the Green Paper for greater coordination of European standard-making have also caused some concern to US industry. The Commission provoked the US by suggesting, in its initial draft, that the EC should vote *en bloc* in the ISO. The idea was dropped from the final draft of the Green Paper.[12]

There is also the problem of establishing any discipline in the US. The various private standard-making bodies are resistant to any control from ANSI. Although there are regional and national model codes for sectors such as building, there is no obligation to follow these and no redress when a city introduces more restrictive or different building regulations. As a result there are, for example, no uniform building regulations across the US comparable with those currently being introduced in the EC. If enforcing even national standards is a problem, the prospects for enforcing internationally agreed standards are pretty bleak. For example, the GATT provisions on technical barriers to trade (see below) are only enforceable for public bodies at the federal level in the US. Neither state nor local authorities are bound by these provisions, and they are therefore free to use technical specifications which discriminate in favour of local suppliers. The utilities can, if they so wish, also refer to national US or industry-specific standards in their specifications for tenderers, thus effectively precluding foreign suppliers. Having said this, the US market is more unified and less fragmented by national design standards than the European market. This means that while the costs of tooling up for the US standard are considerable and represent a form of barrier to market access, any firm once in the US market can sell across the continent, whereas European experience in the utilities has shown that design standards laid down by a network operator can form a major barrier to each national market.

The US system of standard-making is in theory open to all, but in practice it is difficult – and often prohibitively costly – for even large companies that do not have a local US affiliate to follow what is going on in the hundreds of standard-making bodies, let alone actively participate. Transparency is poor because not all the private standards bodies are affiliated to ANSI. In comparison the European standards bodies bring together summaries of all the work in progress in the EC standard-making bodies. Subscription to the newsletters of the four major institutes, which account for the bulk of national standard-making work, thus provides a comprehensive overview.

Third-country issues
Fears in the US that European standards represent an element of 'fortress Europe' must therefore be put into context. A general lack of understanding of the standard-making procedures was at the root of the original fortress Europe claims. It was claimed that the US was banned from participating in European standard-making, while European firms were able to participate in the US process. This is factually correct since only the national standards institutes participate in European standard-

making, except in the case of ETSI, but the issue is more complex in practice. The EC argues that it provides national treatment, which it does, as required in the GATT agreement of 1979. Again, the issue is one of systemic differences between the US and the EC. By asking for a seat at the table of European standard-making the US Secretary of Commerce was in fact asking for more than national treatment. The general message propagated by policy-makers with an imprecise understanding of standard-making was that the Europeans would now be setting standards that would exclude US products. There was initially no recognition that the 'new approach' promised to bring about a major liberalization in the EC. In response to the US request for participation, the Commission and national policy-makers argued that the US should take the ISO more seriously, and that to give the US a seat at the CEN/CENELEC table would risk duplicating the ISO. In 1989 a compromise was found whereby CEN/CENELEC exchange information with ANSI. This went a fair way towards assuaging US concerns but still leaves the domestic problem of how to get the 'pluralistic' US standard-making to operate through ANSI.

In addition to its desire for a seat at the table, the US was concerned that its existing bilateral agreements with individual member states on mutual recognition of certification would not be automatically extended to the EC. The Community argued that it could not commit all its member states to agreements reached between the US (or any other country) and an individual member state. The main concern for US companies was the increased costs of possibly having to go outside the US to get a product certified, if mutual recognition of tests could not be agreed. It was rightly argued that this would mean US companies could face higher costs than their competitors on the European market. From the EC side there was no suggestion that mutual recognition of certification would not, ultimately, be extended to the EC as a whole. This is a legitimate concern and one that has been made more tricky in the past by the lack of an effective coordinated approach to certification and testing in the US. The EC has made it clear that it will recognize only designated testing bodies and that it is seeking some form of reciprocity. But until very recently, with the more active role of the US National Institute of Standards and Technology (NIST) in the accreditation of test houses, there was no coordinated national approach in the US. Legislation (the Fastener Quality Act of 1992) has now begun to address the problem of this lack of a central accreditation of testing bodies that would be sufficient to meet EC requirements on technical and reciprocity grounds.

While mutual recognition of testing and certification is a legitimate issue, the weight it assumed in the US–EC debate is out of all proportion to its importance relative to both the significant liberalizing effect of the EC regime as a whole and the existence of structural impediments to trade resulting from the absence of agreed standards, especially in the US.

After some initial alarm US industry, especially the larger companies with a presence in Europe, recognized the benefits of establishing European standards to replace national standards. But the US concern was re-awakened by the Commission's Green Paper. There is concern, for example among the National Association of Manufacturers (NAM), about the proposed shortening of the period for public comment. Specific reference to cooperation with Central and East European countries is also seen with concern in the US because the adoption of European standards by these countries could discriminate against US suppliers. But the underlying concern is that the emphasis on strengthening European standard-making will result in a weakening of the international standard-making processes. The Commission's response still appears to be that the EC takes the ISO and IEC more seriously than the US and Japanese do and that if the US is really worried it should do more to support existing international standard-making procedures. It remains to be seen how many, if any, of the Commission's proposals will be adopted by the EC.

Multilateral agreements
There are two main multilateral fora, the international standard-making institutions – the ISO and IEC – and the GATT.

The International Organization for Standardization
One of the major reasons for the limited efficacy of the International Organization for Standardization is that it is too slow and cannot keep pace with technological developments. The presence of numerous industrialized and developing countries tends to slow down its work so that it can take many years to agree on a standard. The ISO therefore reflects many of the problems that the EC experienced under its old approach. It also reflects the old EC in the sense that the active countries in standard-making call the tune. In Europe this was the Germans, led by the DIN; in the ISO it is the Europeans. The US rightly argues that the fact that the Europeans can outvote it by 18 to 1 means it has little incentive to participate. The only way of removing this structural weakness would be to give the EC a single vote in the ISO. It is not clear how the EC and EFTA could

be included in one vote unless the vote were given to CEN/CENELEC. The European Commission does not seem to rule this out entirely, although the initial proposals for bloc voting in ISO by the EC member states suggests the EC will not lightly cede its voting advantage. The EC and European standards institutes are, however, keen to see a more effective ISO.

Reform of the ISO is likely to raise further important practical questions for the US. First and foremost it would mean a significant increase in the US financial contribution. At present the individual European institutions carry most of the costs. If their representation were reduced to one vote there would also be a reduction in their contribution. Over eighty per cent of the private standard-making bodies are not even part of ANSI and are resisting its attempts to increase central coordination. There is some doubt whether these companies would be prepared to make the contributions to ANSI that will be needed if the US is to have a more effective and influential input into the ISO.

GATT

The GATT agreement on technical barriers to trade negotiated in the Tokyo round sought to increase transparency by requiring that national technical standards should be notified to the GATT, and, like the EC Information Directive, providing signatories with an opportunity of commenting on the standards proposed by other nations. A period is set aside during which consultations can take place if any signatory feels that the proposed national standard will create technical barriers to trade. Each signatory to the code also has to provide inquiry points, usually the national standards institutions, from which information on technical standards can be obtained. There is even an obligation to use international standards wherever possible. Finally, the national treatment measures provided for fair treatment once a product has crossed the frontier. This does not, however, extend any rights to participation in national standard-making processes.

The GATT code's objectives at the international level are very similar to those of the EC's Information Directive. Indeed both originated in 1980 and both draw on the same philosophical principles. But the GATT code has proved much less effective. Its coverage is, for example, limited to central government because of the political and constitutional difficulties for the US and Canada in binding the sub-federal levels of government. Private standards bodies are also under no obligation to notify standards to GATT. Most important of all, there is no effective proactive enforcement, as there is in the EC, where decisions of the European

Court of Justice, such as in the *Cassis de Dijon* case, have shaped European standards policy.

During the Uruguay round there were negotiations on an improved code on technical barriers to trade. A revised 1990 Agreement on Technical Barriers to Trade at the Brussels ministerial meeting would have been possible had the talks not collapsed.[13] This agreement seeks to provide national treatment in the application of technical regulations by *central* government. In other words, any technical requirements resulting from central government decisions must not discriminate between imported and national products. The agreement provides considerable scope for exceptions on the grounds of national security, human, animal and plant health and 'the environment'. This last exception is significant because many commentators expect environmental standards to become one of the chief future areas of difficulty. The broad exceptions available under the draft agreement suggest that, contrary to the fears of some US environmentalists, there will be little discipline over national environmental standards and thus scope for differences between the EC and the US. Generally, there is more than enough scope for national regulators to find ways around the agreement. For example, there is a requirement to use international standards but exceptions are allowed if these are ineffective or inappropriate. As the US currently appears to find only seventeen ISO standards both effective and appropriate, the chances of a significant increase in international standards as a result of the revised agreement are not encouraging.

More promising, however, are the provisions for a 'code of good practice' for standards bodies. This is required for central government bodies. In addition, the signatory governments are required to take 'all reasonable measures as may be available to them' to ensure that local government and non-governmental standardizing bodies also use the code. The code begins to address the key problems in international standard-making by urging that every effort be made:

(1) to avoid duplication of national and international standards;
(2) to reach agreement on a national consensus (important given the situation in the US);
(3) to provide information on work programmes and standards agreed (this could mean better information on all standard-making bodies in both the EC and the US); and
(4) to allow standardization bodies in other signatories 60 days to comment.

The code appears to be an effort at a compromise to bring the private standards bodies in countries such as the US into the international system. The emphasis of the proposed agreement is, however, on improving the provisions on conformity assessment procedures (i.e. certification and testing procedures). Here it seems to offer real improvements by paving the way towards mutual recognition of conformity assessment.

Progress continued to be made in the run-up to the Brussels meeting. For example, it was agreed that further discussions would be held on applying general GATT dispute settlement procedures to the agreement. This could represent progress because revised dispute settlement procedures promise to be very much more effective than the existing procedures of the 1979 Agreement on Technical Barriers to Trade. Their application to a revised agreement would mean more rapid resolution of disputes on such issues as conformity assessment. On one issue, however, there appears to have been no consensus. This was the extension of the agreement to cover local government, which the EC seeks and to which the US remains opposed.

Conclusions

As in public procurement and to some extent in competition policy, the EC's approach to standard-making is aimed at removing the structural impediments, in the shape of national standards, that are the legacy of past national regulatory policies and at preventing such barriers developing in the future. Here, as with competition, policy is being codified in EC statutes. As EC directives replace national regulation the Community is likely to focus on statutory barriers rather than on structural impediments.

In the US the reverse is the case. The continued reliance on industry standards and the general weakness of public policy in the field of standards mean that technical barriers to market access are more likely to take the form of structural impediments than statutory regulation. In other words, the absence of effective action by public bodies in the US means that structural impediments may exist in the shape of standards determined by a company or companies with a dominant market position. A case in point is telecommunications networks, where the AT&T standard means the costs of market entry can be high. The US industry argues that the US market in telecommunications switching is open because some 30% of the market is taken by Northern Telecom of Canada. But this is not inconsistent with the case that structural impediments exist. Northern Telecom has tooled up for the US market and invested heavily in it.

The approaches to technical standards in the EC and US vary greatly. The European industry, governments and standards bodies have responded to the market-led demand for more standards by reforming their decision-making procedures so as to ensure that agreed European standards can be produced more quickly. In other words, there has been a trend towards reregulation of standards at the European level. The Commission's Green Paper suggests a continuation of this trend. The US has traditionally left standard-making to the market, in the shape of private standard-making bodies controlled by industry. Even if the current efforts to strengthen the coordination of US standard-making and certification are successful, the gap between these two different approaches is likely to continue.

International standard-making has been neglected, especially in the US. Faced with European dominance, the US has retreated and refused to accept standards agreed by the ISO. The EC's 1992 programme and its new approach to standard-making has accentuated the challenge. If the US fails to take international standard-making procedures more seriously the Europeans, led by the EC, will further strengthen their dominance in the field. The general lack of willingness on the part of significant sections of US industry to participate in efforts to reach agreed international standards fits uneasily with the US demand for a greater say in European standard-making. Suspicion of the European dominance may well have led to the relatively low profile adopted by the US in its approach to GATT negotiations on standards. It is interesting to contrast its maximalist positions in areas such as services, investment and agriculture with its much more modest expectations in the negotiations on standards. As with public procurement the US faces a challenging question: whether to extend multilateral discipline to the sub-federal level of government and to accept a more intrusive role for the state in policy-making.

7
CONCLUSIONS

The preceding chapters have shown that systemic differences between the EC and the US will have an important bearing on the debate about how to handle non-tariff barriers, in the form of regulatory policies and structural impediments. Indeed it will be these systemic differences that will define the coastline of any regional trading blocs that emerge. But such differences should not be overplayed. The reefs of non-tariff barriers influenced the shape of commercial diplomacy between the US and the EC during the debates over industrial policy and subsidies in the 1970s. Clearly, systemic differences in the form of structural impediments embedded in the contours of each economy may be harder to deal with, but it should not be forgotten that trade policy over subsidies has done no more than devise ways of containing conflicts resulting from the systemic differences. There has been little convergence of policy. Similar means must be found for containing the conflicts that will result from differences over regulatory policy and structural impediments. The first step towards this objective is to gain a better understanding of the nature of the differences between the EC and the US. These include the nature of the barriers themselves, the federal issue, the role of the state, the degree of intrusiveness acceptable when tackling structural barriers, and attitudes towards adjudication.

Conclusions

The nature of barriers to access

The case-studies have shown that non-statutory barriers are relatively more important in the EC than in the US, where the requirement that actions by public authorities be according to due process contains covert, non-statutory barriers, with the result that statutory barriers to market access are likely to predominate. Multilateral rules are likely to have a more liberalizing effect in countries such as the US, in which statutory barriers predominate. The pressures in the US for concrete results in efforts to remove 'unfair' trade practices in the shape of non-statutory barriers such as structural impediments can therefore be expected to continue. Against this background the 1992 process may reduce the statutory barriers in the EC, but bring the non-statutory barriers into sharper focus. Given the precedent of the SII talks with Japan, it may be difficult for the US administration to contain pressures for action against similar, if less significant, structural impediments in the EC. In order to address structural impediments, not to mention regulatory barriers to trade, US trade diplomacy is likely to be taken beyond the relative safety of *de jure* national treatment and into the uncharted waters of *de facto* national treatment in more and more areas. The EC will, as indicated by its third-country provisions in services and procurement, follow a similar path. As in the past, however, its approach will be more relaxed because with more impediments of its own there will be less domestic pressure for aggressive trade diplomacy of this type.

The federal issue

The US may well be the *demandeur* when it comes to efforts to tackle structural impediments and other non-statutory barriers to market access, but the EC can be expected to press for adequate discipline at the 'sub-federal' level of regulation and policy. The case-studies have revealed just how important this level of policy-making is in determining market access. The further one moves into questions of regulatory policy the greater the relevance of the individual states. In the EC multilateral agreements are binding on all levels of government. In the majority of cases the issue is covered by Community competence; the member states are obliged to implement EC decisions and are responsible for ensuring that sub-national/regional government does also. In the few cases where there is not full Community competence, such as on some investment issues, the member states are signatories, or co-signatories, and are thus bound to implement the agreement. There are also important differences in how the EC and the US deal with 'sub-federal' authorities. In the EC both the 1992 programme and the Single European Act have emphasized *home* country control as a means of dealing with regulations that differ from state to state. In the US *host* state control remains the predominant formula in the areas where the states retain competence, such as in financial services. Some competition among rules has occurred within the US, with the result that state regulation and policies, for example in taxation, have partially – though by no means completely – converged.

But the main systemic difference between the EC and the US is that Congress is reluctant to pass legislation which binds the states as regards foreign commercial relations. Each of the case-studies covered shows individual US states pursuing policies which limit market access; Congress has failed to legislate, not for constitutional reasons but because of political constraints. In contrast the tendency in the EC is towards shifting the relevant legislation to Community level. More importantly, however, mutual recognition and home country control limit the ability of national regulators or policy-makers to insulate their states from the international economy. Host state control does not create this dynamic. Finally, while both the US and the EC will continue to have dualist systems, consisting of policy powers at two relevant levels, the 1992 programme and EC integration in general are forcing a process of dynamic change in the relationship between the two levels within the Community, and this has facililated regulatory reform. By comparison the case-studies covered here show the US dualist system as less able to adapt to the pressures of global economic integration. The US has no equivalent to the 1992 programme; if a North American Free Trade Area is created it will be based on host country control. For example, the agreement on public purchasing in the US–Canada Free Trade Agreement has no effect on the ability of the individual states to continue with their local 'Buy America' provisions. Another example is the US financial services market, where the competence of the individual states has helped to delay regulatory reform, with the result that the market has suffered from the same kind of fragmentation that plagued the EC before the Single European Act. This does not hold for all sectors, however: deregulation in US air services and telecommunications has, after all, been more rapid and more radical than in Europe.

The role of the state
Despite the efforts of (mainly British) Conservative governments during

Conclusions

the 1980s the state, in the sense of public authority, retains a more important role in the economy in Europe than in the US. This systemic difference has long been a source of considerable difficulties, as was seen over the subsidies issue. The Europeans have argued that subsidies are a legitimate policy instrument, while the US has tended to favour prohibition. It can be anticipated that similar difficulties will arise with non-tariff barriers that stem from divergent regulatory policies. As regulatory policy becomes more central to the policy debate than the extent of public ownership, the importance of such systemic differences may decline. However, European governments, and by extension the European Community, are still likely to insist on socio-political objectives being pursued by regulators and thus be at odds with the US. The differences over the role of subsidies, whatever form those take, seem likely to continue all the same, as is clearly happening with Airbus and support for R&D programmes. In some cases regulatory policy acts as a subsidy anyway, as when regulation sanctions cross-subsidization between regulated operations (i.e. those not subject to market competition) and unregulated ones.

The degree of intrusiveness
In parallel with the continuing European propensity to intervene in the economy, a more intrusive approach to dealing with non-statutory barriers is also emerging at the EC level. Home country control and mutual recognition offer a means of tackling regulatory or statutory barriers, but have left many non-statutory barriers and structural impediments untouched. Thus the EC has been obliged to introduce intrusive new regulation in order to open markets that have long been closed as a result of non-statutory barriers. The case of public procurement is an example where the EC has even extended regulation to cover privately owned companies. The standards case also shows how the emphasis in the EC has been on strengthening European public standard-making as a means of removing or preventing structural impediments in the shape of divergent national standards. So intrusive an approach is unacceptable in the US. Both the procurement and standards cases illustrate how the US is unwilling to accept either that structural impediments to market access in the US do exist in these areas, or that government can or should do anything about them.

In one area, however, it is possible to see scope for convergence between the EC and US approaches to dealing with such impediments: this is

114

competition policy. In the past the majority of European governments have used this as a discretionary instrument of national industrial policy. But the EC level of policy is more codified and based on competition criteria. In this field, therefore, the EC is moving towards a more adjudicative and less political approach, which is more compatible with the US approach.

Adjudication and due process

One of the relevant systemic differences is between the US emphasis on due process in public law and the more discretionary European approach. This has meant, for example, that any industry concluding a 'voluntary' export restraint agreement (VER) with a troublesome exporting country has faced the prospect of an anti-trust action in the US. In the EC, by comparison, neither national nor European competition policy has been used against VERs. At the multilateral level the US emphasis on due process and legalism has resulted in the US supporting adjudicative means of resolving disputes, even if it has not always been prepared to implement the result in the shape of GATT panel decisions. This was unacceptable to the Europeans, who until recently resisted the use of adjudication within GATT, arguing that the resolution of significant disputes represented policy choices and therefore could not be left to adjudication. Traditionally the EC has resisted the establishment of GATT panels, while the US has wished to see far more. European trade officials argue that the EC was cautious in establishing panels but implemented the decisions, while the US was quick to establish panels and slower to implement their decisions.

The creation of a codified European legal regime, however, changes this. In many instances EC legislation in the form of directives or regulations means the introduction either of statutory provisions resulting in fewer discretionary powers, as in the case of merger control, or of a system of codified law where there was previously nothing, as in contract award procedures for public procurement. At a multilateral level the EC has also made a complete U-turn and come out in favour of stronger adjudicative procedures. This is clearly reflected in the EC's support for a strengthened GATT dispute settlement procedure which removes the power of any single Contracting Party to block a GATT panel report, and is consistent with the greater use of qualified majority voting within the EC.

A challenge for US and EC policy-makers

These systemic differences pose a challenge for policy-makers on both sides of the Atlantic. As Chapter 2 showed, there is a growing degree of market interpenetration and economic interdependence across the Atlantic, as well as worldwide. Companies operating under different home-based regimes are therefore competing across borders. If the economic benefits of increased trade and investment are to be gained, policy-makers must find ways of accommodating such systemic differences. If they fail the political pressures may result in limits being set on further economic integration.

For the US the challenge is twofold. First, the development of a distinctive European approach to accommodating intra-EC systemic differences means that the US will be less able to shape the multilateral system in its own image. There have been differences between the US and European (or for that matter Japanese) approaches to commercial policy in the past. As the leading economy of the West, however, the US was able to exercise its hegemony and shape the structure of the GATT rules. Even though US influence faded relative to that of the EC during the 1970s and 1980s it was still able to shape the agenda and the outcome of multilateral trade talks by a proactive stance and the fact that the EC, and still less Japan, was unable to articulate a clear alternative approach.

What has changed is that the EC has now developed a new approach to market liberalization, one that is of direct relevance to the kinds of barriers to market access that will be the focus of commercial diplomacy in the 1990s. This is the application of *competition among rules*, based on mutual recognition and home country control. When it comes to dealing with regulatory barriers to trade, such an approach offers distinct advantages. The alternative is the *approximation of national regulation*. Given the systemic differences approximation is unlikely to be easy and the tendency will be to use some form of 'reciprocity' based on such concepts as 'equivalent competitive opportunity'. The danger is that reciprocity can all too readily become a means of introducing restrictions on market access. In comparison competition among rules offers, in principle, a means of not only accommodating different regulatory systems but also helping to promote convergence. Finally, by leaving *formal* sovereignty unaffected it avoids the political difficulties of ceding sovereignty.

The EC has also developed a coherent approach to structural impediments based on a supranational competition policy and directives aimed at addressing the structural impediments which are legacies of past industrial policies, such as procurement and standards. The case of standards in fact shows how the more intrusive European approach of dealing with technical barriers to trade has come to dominate international fora. When the US companies were strong enough to impose industry standards on the rest of the world this could be ignored. But as the US sensitivity to the standards issue in the 1992 programme shows, it is no longer possible to ignore what the EC is doing. It must be stressed that extending the competition among rules, let alone supranational competition policy, to the multilateral level is still only a theoretical possibility. One of the main challenges for the EC is to articulate and project these approaches effectively in the multilateral debate.

The second reason why the EC poses a challenge to the US is, as already indicated, its growing influence. The EC already accounts for 33 per cent of world trade. The 1992 programme and the moves towards economic and monetary union promise an increased degree of cohesion. The Community process and the *acquis communautaire* are also influencing other countries in Europe. Even before the conclusion of the European Economic Area negotiations, EFTA countries were aligning their legislation and regulations to those of the EC. The Central and East European countries are also using the EC rather than the US as a model when it comes to establishing regulatory policies; for example, EC technical standards are likely to be adopted there. In the monetary field countries such as Sweden, Norway and Finland are pegging their currencies to the ecu, and after monetary union the ecu could well be preferred to the dollar by Central and Eastern Europe. The net effect of this magnetic effect of the Community process is a strengthening of the European 'regulatory sphere of influence'.[1]

The EC also faces the challenge of finding some way of ensuring that its internal dynamic is consistent with an external policy. Its application of competition among rules has proved highly effective in creating an internal dynamism, but the EC has yet to project such dynamism into its external economic relations. This is in part because of the limited importance attributed to external trade relations by national politicians and European business. There is some truth in the US criticism here. But it is also because the EC approach cannot be simply extended beyond the Community, as the agricultural débâcle in the autumn of 1990 showed only too painfully.

The US response

The US response to these challenges has been to seek solutions on three

117

planes: multilateral, bilateral and unilateral. First, the US has, as in past decades, sought to create *multilateral* rules governing the new issues in trade relations. It is the US which has been the most proactive in bringing the new issues of services, investment and intellectual property rights into the GATT negotiations. It has been better than the EC or Japan at initiating proposals and presenting negotiating positions. But the EC has been able to accept the agenda set by the US and effectively represent its own interests. Setting the agenda may have advantages but it has not enabled the US to dictate the rules. Consequently situations arise such as that in services, in which the US has made all the running in the negotiations, only to back off at the last minute. In recent years, and especially during the course of the Uruguay round, US objectives have emphasized concrete improvements in market access rather than establishing multilateral rules. The US support for the multilateral system has thus become more conditional upon the GATT delivering real improvements in market access. If this does not look like happening recourse to bilateral or unilateral means is considered legitimate.

Second, the US has turned to *bilateral* arrangements such as the creation of free trade agreements, first with Canada and now to include Mexico in a North American Free Trade Area. There are also efforts to strengthen links with Latin America through the 'Enterprise for the Americas' initiative. In addition to the benefits of dynamic trade creation, the US is also able to dominate such a grouping in a way that it can no longer do in the multilateral system.

Third, the US has used remedies written into domestic trade legislation over the past 20 years as a means of pressing *unilaterally* for improved market access. As the case-studies have shown, the US has become more and more frustrated with the multilateral approach, and the administration has found it harder and harder to contain pressures within Congress for unilateral action. The use of Section 301 of the Trade Act is the best example of such unilateral measures.

How effective are the multilateral instruments?

The GATT

In the past GATT has offered a set of reasonably clear principles, such as national treatment, non-discrimination and mfn status. These were not always complied with and numerous exceptions were made, but they facilitated fairly clear rules against which to assess national trade measures. The case-studies discussed above suggest that these principles are no longer seen to be adequate. Both the US and the EC have been forced to go beyond *de jure* national treatment and pursue policies based on *de facto* national treatment. This was to be expected because national treatment cannot ensure market access when regulatory policies and practices diverge. The US has been more aggressive in its forays beyond national treatment because the relative importance of non-statutory/structural impediments and regulatory barriers in Japan and the EC means that a system based strictly on national treatment would not deliver the results the domestic US constituencies are expecting.

Japan has understandably criticized this drift from GATT rules and the growth of 'results-based' trade policy, because the relative importance of non-statutory barriers in its own market has meant that Japan could comply with the multilateral rules of national treatment and non-discrimination, with little fear of it having much effect on market access. The EC, and even more the US, have therefore found *de jure* national treatment is not sufficient. The GATT has always provided enough flexibility to deal with such problems. It is, after all, based on the principle of broad – as opposed to sectoral – reciprocity. In the GATS negotiations on services efforts are being made at applying the GATT principles to each sector and in so doing seeking to interpret how the principles can be adapted to cope with the different circumstances. As Chapter 3 shows, the draft sectoral annex for financial services includes reference to 'equivalent competitive opportunities' – a form of wording used in EC and US reciprocity provisions.

The difficulty is how to assess when 'equivalent competitive opportunities' exist where there are different regulatory systems. There have been similar problems in the past. Again the case of subsidies in the Tokyo round illustrates the point. The approach adopted then was to produce a text of an agreement, which frankly papered over most of the systemic differences, in the hope that subsequent GATT 'case law' would fill them in later. But the differences were too great and the dispute settlement provisions too weak, with the result that another attempt had to be made in the Uruguay round. It would be optimistic to assume that the current negotiations on the new issues will be considerably more successful. Certainly the case-studies covered here suggest that systemic differences will continue for some time. When it comes to structural impediments the effort to reach multilateral rules on what governments should do to ensure transparent competitive markets has not even begun. Whatever the outcome of the Uruguay round, therefore, there will be a need to continue to work on agreed definitions if each major player is not to determine unilaterally what 'equivalent competitive access' is and what should be done if it is not provided by a trading partner. This should in no way underestimate the need for a successful conclusion of the Uruguay round. This will be essential – although not sufficient – if the GATT multilateral system is to retain credibility.

The OECD

Even if the Uruguay round is a complete success it will only address some of the regulatory barriers to market access and leave most of the non-statutory barriers untouched. For some time now there have been suggestions, mainly among US trade policy analysts, that the group of like-minded industrialized countries should press ahead with the more ambitious task of opening regulated markets – the assumption being that greater progress could be made in the OECD than in the more hetero-geneous GATT. Pressure for such a 'GATT of the like-minded' is especially strong in the US. Such a route is, however, not without problems. First, the OECD countries may not be so like-minded after all. The preceding chapters have illustrated some important systemic differences between the two key players, the US and the EC. It was as much these differences as any difficulties caused by the developing countries that led to the failure to reach agreement on GATT in Brussels; indeed the North–South confrontation which had been anticipated during the round did not materialize. Another problem is that any plurilateral approach in the OECD must be consistent with GATT. At a time when the developing countries and former state-trading countries are actively seeking to become members of the international trading system, it would be economic and political folly for the OECD, even if slightly expanded, to strike out alone. Finally, there is a question as to whether the OECD is the right forum in which to draft binding rules.

The OECD can, however, go on playing an important role. Systemic differences will persist. Early or rapid convergence is unlikely. There will therefore be a competition among different regulatory spheres of influence at a global level. The EC experience with the analogous competition among rules suggests that there are two preconditions for successfully dealing with different regimes: market pressure and an institutional infrastructure, which in the EC takes the form of directives implementing home country control and harmonizing essential minimum requirements, backed up by supranational institutions and the supremacy of European law. The latter represents a loss of sovereignty that few countries outside Europe are ready to accept. But as the investment and financial services case-studies showed, a form of *de facto* competition among rules does operate at an international level, as a result of economic interdependence and market pressure. The role of the OECD should therefore be to promote this process, and it would not be without precedent. The OECD codes on investment have, as shown in Chapter 4, worked in this way by bringing peer pressure to bear. They have even begun to address 'impediments' to investment, i.e. non-statutory barriers to access. A strengthening of the GATT as a forum for dealing with new issues in trade and investment might also be possible if the Uruguay round can be successfully concluded. The EC has, in fact, proposed the creation of a Multilateral Trade Organization, which would serve the purpose of bringing the GATT and the GATS under one roof and also provide a stronger secretariat and uniform dispute settlement procedures.

Bilateral relations
The EC and the US have also made efforts to improve bilateral relations. For historical reasons there are many links between policy-makers across the Atlantic. In addition there are extensive private-sector links, as illustrated by the degree of investment (see Chapter 2). The intensification of European integration has further strengthened ties between the US and the Community institutions. The clearest expression of the desire to strengthen the policy linkages to match the high degree of economic interdependence was the signing of the Atlantic Declaration in November 1990.[2] This originated in speeches by President Bush in Boston in May 1989, and by the US Secretary of State, James Baker, in Berlin in December of the same year, calling for closer links between the Community and the US. More important than the declaration, however, has been a considerable strengthening of the transatlantic institutional connections over recent years. In March 1990 it was agreed that each President of the Council would meet with the US President. For its part the Commission has established that its President will also meet with the US President and his leading cabinet officials twice a year. In addition, European foreign ministers will meet with the US Secretary of State, and the regular biannual meetings between the EC Commission and the US cabinet will also continue. Last, but by no means least, the European Parliament and Congress have worked hard at strengthening their links; it was a joint meeting in January 1989 which suggested the establishment

of a bilateral dispute settlement procedure similar to that established by the US–Canada Free Trade Agreement.

On a more functional basis there have also been proposals for closer cooperation between the Commission and the US government in the fields of competition policy, research and development, education, etc. In standard-making, as shown in Chapter 6, bilateral consultation procedures have been strengthened. In financial services there is a long history of close links between national regulators, especially between the British and the Americans, which has provided a sound base for the EC–US dialogue.

The way forward
The answer to the problems in tackling the new market access issues, given the systemic differences, lies in employing all three means: multilateral, bilateral and plurilateral. An effective multilateral framework is necessary if a general growth in bilateralism is to be avoided. GATT has always been a mixture: its function is to provide a multilateral reference for bilateral agreements and to ensure that the benefits of bilateral agreements are extended to third countries by means of the principle of mfn status. Regardless of what happens on the bilateral or plurilateral front it is therefore essential to make progress in defining GATT rules and strengthening GATT disciplines. To achieve this the Uruguay round must be brought to a successful conclusion. The primary precondition for this is that there be some convergence between the expectations of the US on the one hand and most of the other Contracting Parties on the other. US negotiators argue that it is not that the US has expectations that are too high but that the others have set their sights too low. But, as argued in Chapter 2, it is a difference not simply in the *level* of expectations but in the *kind* of expectation. The US expectations are predominantly about concrete results for US exporters; those of the EC, Japan and many others also include extending GATT rules to the new issues and strengthening GATT disciplines. If GATT is to provide a multilateral framework of rules there must be progress on the latter, but for the US Congress to support the final outcome of the round there must also be actual market-opening.

However successful the Uruguay round is, it will not resolve all the market access issues. Pressure will therefore continue and there will be benefits in channelling it through such bodies as the OECD and indeed bilateral talks, provided no action is taken which undermines the multilateral system. The US administration can be expected to press for something to be done in the OECD. The most appropriate area of work would be to look at the nature of new barriers to market access in the OECD countries. This would in effect extend the SII-type approach to a plurilateral level. But it would be unfortunate if expectations were raised too high. The OECD will not be able to produce quick results on market access any more easily than the GATT, especially in those areas in which the lack of progress in the Uruguay round has resulted from differences between the US and the EC. Nor is it the appropriate body for concluding binding agreements. Rather, the participants should seek to augment the effects of market forces in bringing about a *de facto* competition among rules approach.

NOTES

Chapter 1

1 See William Diebold, Jr., *Industrial Policy as an International Issue*, McGraw-Hill for the Council on Foreign Relations/1980s Project, New York, 1980.
2 See Albert Bressand, 'Beyond interdependence: 1992 as a global challenge', *International Affairs*, vol. 66, no. 1, January 1990.

Chapter 2

1 Glennon Harrison, *European Community Trade and Investment with the United States*, Congressional Research Service, CRS 90–128 E, Washington DC, 1990.
2 Ibid.
3 A. DiLullo and Obie Whichard, 'US International Sales and Purchases of Services', in US Department of Commerce, *Survey of Current Business*, Washington DC, September 1990.
4 US Department of Commerce, *Survey of Current Business*, Washington DC, August 1990.
5 On the question of global trends in foreign direct investment and investment flows into the EC, see DeAnne Julius, *Global Companies and Public Policy: The Growing Challenge of Foreign Direct Investment*, Chatham House Papers, RIIA/Pinter, London, 1990.
6 See US Department of Commerce, *Survey of Current Business*, June 1990, Table 5.
7 US Department of Commerce, *Survey of Current Business*, July 1990.

Notes

8 See, for example, the Reciprocal Trade and Investment Act (S144) of 1983. For the debate on the issues, see Reciprocal Trade and Investment Act Hearing before the Subcommittee on International Trade of the Committee of Finance, US Senate, 98–11, March 1983.

9 See Stephen Woolcock, Michael Hodges and Kristin Schreiber, *Britain, Germany and 1992: The Limits of Deregulation*, Chatham House Papers, RIIA/Pinter, London, 1991.

10 See, for example, Hans van der Ven in Jeffrey Hart, Hans van der Ven and Stephen Woolcock, *Interdependence in the Post-multilateral Era*, University Press of America, Boston and London, 1985.

11 See paper by Peter Yeo, *Congressional Views on 1992*, at RIIA study group, mimeo, May 1990.

12 See European Commission, *Europe 1992: Europe World Partner in Information*, Commission Spokesman's Service, P–117, 19 October 1988.

13 See Hart, van der Ven and Woolcock, op. cit.

14 See 'Telecommunications Trade', Title I, Subtitle C, Point 4 of Omnibus Trade and Competitiveness Act of 1988, in *Overview and Compilation of US Trade Statutes*, 1989 edition, Committee of Ways and Means, US House of Representatives (101–14), 18 September 1989, p. 763.

15 See International Trade Commission, *The Effects of Greater Economic Integration within the European Community on the United States*, Washington DC, July 1989. There have been three follow-up reports, in March 1990, September 1990 and March 1991.

16 See, for example, *Europe 1992: Administration Views*, Hearings before Subcommittees on Europe and the Middle East and on International Economic Policy and Trade of the Committee on Foreign Affairs, US House of Representatives, 20 February 1990.

17 There are annual reports on barriers to trade; see, for example, *1990 National Trade Estimate Report on Foreign Trade Barriers*, Office of the US Trade Representative, Government Printing Office, Washington DC, 1990.

18 For the latest report see Services of the Commission of the European Communities, *Report on the United States Trade Barriers and Unfair Practices 1991: Problems of Doing Business with the US*. In a further illustration of how trade policy measures are imitated by others, Japan has now followed suit and produced a report on the 'unfair' practices of both the EC and US; see the Fair Trade Centre, *Report on Unfair Trade Policies and Practices, Trade Barriers and GATT Obligations in the US, EC and Canada*, Tokyo, June 1991.

19 See Stephen Woolcock, *The Uruguay Round: Issues for the European Community and the United States*, RIIA Discussion Paper No. 31, RIIA, London, October 1990. For a more comprehensive treatment of the issues see Jeffrey Schott (ed.), *Completing the Uruguay Round: A Results-oriented Approach to the GATT Trade Negotiations*, Institute for

Notes

International Economics, Washington DC, September 1990.

20 See Sidney Golt, *The GATT Negotiations 1986–90: Origins, Issues and Prospects*, British–North American Committee, London, 1986, for a general history of the round.

21 See Philip Hayes, *Foreign Direct Investment: Will the Uruguay Round Make a Difference?*, RIIA Discussion Paper No. 25, RIIA, London, May 1990, for details of the TRIMs issue.

22 Although there is no scope for a case-study of market access issues in agriculture, some coverage is essential because of the negative impact of the difficulties in reaching an agreement in this sector on EC–US relations within the round and beyond. For a more detailed treatment of agriculture, see J. Rollo, *Agriculture in the Uruguay Round: Foundations for Success*, RIIA Discussion Paper No. 26, RIIA, London, June 1990.

23 This applied to the round in general but especially to agriculture. Such statements were made before the round was launched in Punta del Este, as well as during the round, e.g. in the run-up to the Houston summit of July 1990.

24 For details of the mid-term review meeting see Jilyan Kelly and Stephen Woolcock, 'The price of false expectations', *The World Today*, vol. 45, no. 6, June 1989.

25 See speech to the Institute of Directors by Ambassador Carla Hills, reported in *The Financial Times*, 4 June 1991.

26 Ibid.

27 Eurostat Annual Foreign Trade Statistics, 1990, p. 34.

Chapter 3

1 For a description of the sector and the issues in trade in services, see GATT, *Trade in Financial Services*, Note by the Secretariat, 4 September 1989.

2 Bank for International Settlements, 59th Annual Report, 1989.

3 It has been legally possible for him to engage in such *assurance sauvage*, provided he goes direct and does not expect any cover under German prudential insurance measures.

4 In other words, the value of all securities (equity) capital on the Japanese securities markets (stock exchanges) is equivalent to 92% of Japanese GNP. See *World Bank Development Report 1989*.

5 See 'Financial Services' in Stephen Woolcock, Michael Hodges and Kristin Schreiber, *Britain, Germany and 1992: The Limits of Deregulation*, Chatham House Papers, RIIA/Pinter, London, 1991.

6 See Chapter 6, pp. 95–6 for a description of the *Cassis de Dijon* case. The ECJ case in point here was the so-called Schleicher case of 1987, in which the ECJ ruled, in favour of the Commission and against five member states, that German insurance regulatory authorities could not use national

126

regulation to prevent a broker seeking insurance in London. For details see Woolcock et al., op. cit., p. 83.

7 See Council Directive 89/646/EEC, *Official Journal*, L 386, 30 December 1989.

8 See *Amended Proposal for a Council Directive on Investment Services in the Securities Field*, OJ C 42/7, 22 February 1990.

9 See the Third Non-life Insurance Directive, the so-called framework directive, COM(90)348, OJ C244, 28 September 1990.

10 See proposed Third Life Insurance Directive, COM(91)57, April 1991.

11 Council Directive 86/635/EEC, 8 December 1986, on the annual accounts and consolidated accounts of banks and other financial institutions, *Official Journal*, L 372, 31 December 1986.

12 See Thomas Bayard and Kimberly Ann Elliot, *Reciprocity and Retaliation: An Evaluation of Aggressive Trade Policies*, Institute of International Economics, Washington DC, forthcoming, 1992.

13 This is accepted on both sides of the Atlantic. See, for example, evidence by various US commentators and European bankers in *Oversight Hearings on the European Community's 1992 Programme* before the House subcommittee on financial institutions and supervision, regulation and insurance of the Committee on Banking Finance and Urban Affairs, serial No. 101–53, September 1989.

14 See, for example, the evidence of Mr Johnson, Vice-Chairman of the Federal Reserve, in *Oversight Hearings*, op. cit.

15 See European Commission, *Reports on Competition Policy*, annual.

16 European Commission, *Nineteenth Report on Competition Policy*, Brussels, 1990, p. 223.

17 See Lipp Dresdner Bank in *Oversight Hearings*, op. cit.

18 This section draws on the US Treasury Department study *Modernizing the Financial System: Recommendations for Safer, More Competitive Banks*, Washington DC, February 1991.

19 Seven foreign bank holding companies were 'grandfathered', i.e. allowed to continue to operate the bank holding companies they had established.

20 See statement by Willian Seidman, Chairman, Federal Deposit Insurance Corporation, in *Oversight Hearings*, op. cit., p. 7.

21 See Carter H. Golembe and David S. Holland, 'Banking and Securities', in Gary Clyde Hufbauer (ed.), *Europe 1992: An American Perspective*, The Brookings Institution, Washington DC, 1990.

22 *Modernizing the Financial System*, op. cit., XVIII–26.

23 The assets of foreign offices of US banks fell from $390bn in 1983 to $318bn in 1988, and the number of offices from 916 to 849.

24 See Lawrence R. Uhlick, 'Implications for the United States of the Integrated Financial Market in Europe After 1992', at the RIIA Conference 'Goodbye to Fortress Europe', mimeo, March 1990.

25 See *Modernizing the Financial System*, op. cit. The proposals were followed by draft legislation.

26 Ibid.

27 At the time of writing it remains unclear what form legislation will take. Both House and Senate have, for example, thrown out the requirement for foreign banks to establish FSHCs.

28 See *The Financial Times*, 2 May 1991.

29 See *The Financial Times*, 19 July 1991.

30 See Sydney Golt, *Trade Issues in the Mid-1980s*, British-North American Committee, London, 1982, p. 54.

31 This comes through clearly in the negotiating mandate given to the European Commission by the Council of (Foreign) Ministers in June 1986.

32 At the Brussels ministerial meeting of the Uruguay round, progress was made towards a compromise, following a movement by the US on time-limited exceptions from mfn, but the meeting collapsed when no agreement was reached on agriculture.

33 See OECD, *Liberalization of Capital Movements and Financial Services in the OECD Area*, Paris, 1990.

34 For a sophisticated case in favour of OECD-type discussions using a combination of home and host country control, see Sydney Key, 'International Trade in Banking Services: A Conceptual Framework', Federal Reserve, mimeo, August 1990.

Chapter 4

1 See OECD, *Controls and Impediments Affecting Inward Direct Investment in the OECD Member Countries*, Paris, 1987.

2 Recent work by the US Bureau of Economic Analysis suggests that this is not the result of foreign companies buying up US assets. Revised figures for the stock of direct investment based on current values show that the US still has a surplus of foreign assets. The net deficit comes from heavy sales of debt to finance the US budget deficit. See *The Financial Times*, 10 July 1991.

3 It is interesting to note the link between this action and the various 'Buy America' provisions introduced for bearings. Although bearings are clearly needed to keep the wheels of the military machine rolling, the link suggests that focused lobbying also had an effect, and that the domestic industry sought any means available to get relief from import competition.

4 See Edward Graham and Michael Ebert, 'Direct Foreign Investment and National Security: Fixing the Exon–Florio Process', Institute for International Economics, mimeo, 1991.

5 See *The Financial Times*, 18 June 1991.

6 Democrat Congressman Mel Levine, the sponsor of one of the bills, quoted in *Le Monde*, 22 May 1991.

7   See Christopher Layton, *Cross-frontier Mergers in Europe: How Can Governments Help?*, Bath University Press, Bath, 1973.
8   See OECD, *International Mergers and Competition Policy*, Paris, 1988.
9   See European Commission, *Reports on Competition Policy*.
10 See *The Financial Times*, 30 August 1990.
11 Merger Control Regulation 4064/89 EEC, 21 December 1989, Article 2(3).
12 The first few cases looked at by the Commission were allowed through, but the real test case is probably still to come. See *The Financial Times*, 28 May 1991.
13 See Coopers and Lybrand for the Department of Trade and Industry, *Barriers to Takeover in the European Community*, HMSO, London, October 1989.
14 Ibid.
15 For a treatment of these issues see Stephen Woolcock, *Corporate Governance in the Single European Market*, RIIA Discussion Paper No. 32, RIIA, London, October 1990.
16 Ibid.
17 See OECD Code on the Liberalization of Capital Movements, List A, Inward Investment.
18 See OECD, *International Investment and Multilateral Enterprises: National Treatment for Foreign-controlled Enterprises*, Paris, 1985, p. 9.
19 Ibid.
20 See Table 4.1 above for the list in summary form for selected countries.
21 This has covered insurance, banking and securities; see, for example, OECD, *Liberalization of Capital Movements and Financial Services in the OECD Area*, Paris, 1990.
22 For its part the Community, at the suggestion of the European Commission and with the support of the member states, wishes to become a signatory of the Code. This would mean EC, national as well as sub-national authorities would be bound by it.
23 The European Commission speaks for the member states in the OECD on issues covered by Community competence, such as agriculture, trade policy and national treatment. It participates in much of the OECD work and EC positions are coordinated beforehand, but it is the individual member states that vote, not the EC.

Chapter 5

1   See GATT, *Multilateral Trade Negotiations Agreement on Government Procurement*, Geneva, April 1979.
2   See, for example, *Communication from the Commission to the Council on an Action Programme for Public Procurement in the Community*, COM (86)375, 1986.
3   See Directive 70/32/EEC, *Official Journal of the European Communities*,

L13 1970 as revised in Directive 77/62/EEC OJ L13 1977 for supplies; and Directives 71/304 and 71/305/EEC OJ L185 of 1971 for works. The supplies directive was again revised in March 1988 (Directive 88/295/EEC OJ L127 1988) and the works directive in July 1989 (Directive 89/440/EEC, OJ L210 1989).

4 See *Council Directive on the Coordination of Laws, Regulations and Administrative Provisions Relating to the Application of Review Procedures to the Award of Public Supply and Public Works Contracts* of December 1989 (Directive 89/665/EEC OJ L395).

5 See *Council Directive Coordinating the Laws, Regulations and Administrative Provisions Relating to the Application of Community Rules on the Procurement Procedures of Entities in the Water, Energy, Transport and Telecommunications Sectors, Official Journal L297, 29 October 1990.*

6 See *Proposal for a Council Directive Coordinating the Laws, Regulations and Administrative Provisions Relating to the Application of Community Rules on the Procurement Procedures of Entities Operating in Water, Energy, Transport and Telecommunications Sectors*, COM(90) 297, *Official Journal C216*, 31 August 1990.

7 See *Proposal for a Council Directive Relating to the Coordination of Procedures on the Award of Service Contracts*, COM(90) 372, OJ C23, 31 January 1991.

8 For a more detailed treatment, see 'Public Procurement' in Woolcock et al., *Britain, Germany and 1992: The Limits of Deregulation*, Chatham House Papers, RIIA/Pinter, London, 1991.

9 See Annex IA of *Proposal for a Council Directive Relating to the Coordination of Procedures on the Award of Public Services Contracts*, COM(90)372, 31 October 1990.

10 Political agreement on a common position on this directive was reached in the Internal Market Council meeting of 18 June 1991.

11 Non-warlike purchasing by defence establishments is included in the EC Supplies Directive and the GATT GPA. See the revised GATT agreement of 1988 for a list of defence equipment covered.

12 This is not seen as helpful by potential US suppliers, who believe it will introduce uncertainty rather than flexibility.

13 See Commission of the European Communities, *The Cost of Non-Europe*, Brussels, 1988; particularly 'Basic findings', in Volume 1, *Executive Summary*, and Chapter 3, 'Public purchasing', p. 7.

14 See Services of the European Commission, *Report on United States Trade Barriers and Unfair Trade Practices*, Brussels, 1990, p. 23.

15 See National Electrical Manufacturers' Association, 'Identification of priority practices that should be considered with respect to section 301 of the Trade Act of 1974, as amended', submitted to the Section 301

Committee Office of the USTR, March 1989 (unpublished).
16 See *The Omnibus Trade and Competitiveness Act of 1988: An Analysis*, Steptoe and Johnson, Attorneys at Law, Washington DC, November 1988.
17 See Woolcock et al., op. cit.
18 See report in Office of the United States Trade Representative, *1990 National Trade Estimate Report on Foreign Trade Barriers*, 1990.

Chapter 6

1 This distinction between standards, which are 'voluntary' in all countries, and technical regulations is crucial, especially in understanding the EC's 'new approach'.
2 The European standards institutions are not publicly owned. They are private bodies which fulfil functions in the public interest. For example, DIN is funded entirely by contributions from its voluntary members and sales of services, but it is recognized as fulfilling a very important function for the German economy.
3 See Commission of the European Communities, *Green Paper on The Development of European Standardization: Action for Faster Technological Integration in Europe*, COM(90)456, 8 October 1990.
4 See Resolution of the Council of 7 May 1985, *Official Journal*, C136, 4 October 1985. It is argued, in British circles, that the origin of this approach was the 1982 British White Paper on International Standards and Competitiveness drawn up while Lord Cockfield was in the British Department of Trade and Industry.
5 See 'Technical Standards' in Stephen Woolcock, Michael Hodges and Kristin Schreiber, *Britain, Germany and 1992: The Limits of Deregulation*, Chatham House Paper, RIIA/Pinter, London, 1991.
6 As a result Germany tried to block some of the decisions based on the new approach but was outvoted.
7 *Green Paper*, op. cit., p. 34 (author's parenthesis).
8 See Commission of the European Communities, *Global Approach to Certification and Testing*, COM(89)209, 24 July 1989.
9 For a summary of the US position, see *Business America*, 19 June 1989.
10 This experience led to pressure for the Open Systems Interconnect (OSI) approach, which seeks to establish a 'genuine agreed standard' on computer system architecture that will enable all products to be interconnected with each other without being obliged to follow an industry standard.
11 Partly in response to the challenge posed by the Europeans, a number of US trade associations, such as the National Electrical Society of Automobile Engineers, have committed themselves to a more active input into the ISO.
12 For a summary of US concerns, see United States International Trade

Commission, *The Effects of Greater Economic Integration within the European Community on the United States: Third Follow-up Report*, March 1991, pp. 4–8.
13 See draft final act embodying the results of the Uruguay round of multilateral trade negotiations, GATT Trade Negotiations Committee, MTN.TNC/W/35, 26 November 1990 (Special Distribution).

Chapter 7
1 I am indebted to John Richardson of the European Commission for a clear explanation of this concept at one of the RIIA project study groups.
2 See Stephen Woolcock, *Mapping Transatlantic Links*, paper for RIIA study group, mimeo, September 1991.